From the Light of the Qur'ān

A Spiritual Explanation of The Chapter of Sincerity

Tafsīru 'l-Qur'ānu 'l-Karīm

Sūratu 'l- Ikhlāṣ (112)

Shaykh Muḥammad Hishām Kabbānī

Edited and Annotated
by
Professor Paul Hardy, PhD.

Institute for Spiritual and Cultural Advancement

Published by
Institute for Spiritual and Cultural Advancement

17195 Silver Pkwy., #401

Fenton, MI 48430

ISBN 1-930409-42-7

Library of Congress Cataloging-in-Publication Data

Kabbani, Shaykh Muhammad Hisham.

p. cm.

ISBN 1-930409-2942-7

بسم الله الرحمن الرحيم

قُلْ هُوَ اللَّهُ أَحَدٌ

اللَّهُ الصَّمَدُ

لَمْ يَلِدْ وَلَمْ يُولَدْ

وَلَمْ يَكُن لَّهُ كُفُوًا أَحَدٌ

Say! He is Allāh the Unique;
Allāh, the Self-Sufficient,
Upon whom creatures depend,
Who did not beget and was not begotten,
Equal to Him is not anyone.

Contents

Introduction

The subject of the present commentary is on *Sūratu 'l-Ikhlāṣ* or the *Chapter of Single-Hearted Sincerity*. "*Ikhlāṣ*," like the majority of Arabic words, are built up from three letters that convey a word's basic meaning. It makes no difference in what form a word appears. That is, it makes no difference whether it comes in the form of a verbal noun (*maṣdar*) like "*ikhlāṣ*," a finite verb in the present, past or future, a noun, participle, etc. The meaning of the three root letters is always preserved. "*Ikhlāṣ*" is based then on the three Arabic letters, *KH-L-Ṣ*. Together, they carry the meaning "to purify" or "to refine" from all impurities. The very concept of refining and purifying signifies the removing all impurities, leaving nothing but the very essence of that which was sought, which, in this case, is Allāh. Thus, whoever knows Allāh and affirms His Oneness reaches the level of purity or sincerity of heart.

"Purity of heart," it has been said "is to will one thing wholly." And the one who achieves that level is described in Arabic with the adjective, "*mukhliṣ*," that is, sincere. The virtue of single-hearted devotion to Allāh goes to the heart of the religion of Islam. This is hardly surprising. So it is not surprising that tradition holds that reading this chapter just once equals a reading of the entire Qur'ān. For the Qur'ān in its essence is a totally uncompromising proclamation of Divine Unity.

Now the Qur'ān was revealed in a world where God's unity had long been a burning issue. In fact, is the final intervention in a debate between polytheists and monotheists that had been going on for thousands of years. The Qur'ān, of course, summarizes many points of that debate as it existed among the ancient Hebrews, Egyptians, and Christians in the Greco-Roman world.

The prophets, of course, played the largest role in arguing for Divine Unity against the polytheists in those various civilizations.

With the final Prophet, Muḥammad ﷺ came the descent of *Sūratu 'l- Ikhlāṣ*. And in its amazing verses the peoples of antiquity found the problems raised in their controversies resolved in a new and unprecedented way. It removed the darkness of idolatry enshrined not only in their various religions, but in the social practices of their societies. It swept away the clouds of polytheism produced within the souls of its practitioners and offered them a chance to enter a spiritual dimension never dreamed of before that time and unsurpassed even today. In short, the Qur'ān in general and *Sūratu 'l- Ikhlāṣ* in particular, became instruments of social and spiritual regeneration.

That is why the original hearers *Sūratu 'l- Ikhlāṣ* found it persuasive. And through its mighty power they were able to vanquish the numerous idols they saw erected in the temples of the external world but also those more hidden idols concealed within the interior regions of their own souls. They found it convincing not simply because it declares God to be one and not two or three, however powerful that declaration might be. Its persuasive force penetrates much deeper. It comes to fruition in the actualizing of the Muslim twofold testimony of faith or *shahāda* formula "*Lā ilāha illa 'l-Lāh*" or "There is no divinity (or reality or absolute) save the sole Divinity (or Reality or Absolute)" and "*Muḥammadun rasūlu 'l-Lāh*" or "Muḥammad is the Messenger (Spokesman or Intermediary or Manifestation) of the sole Divinity (or Reality or Absolute)."

The following commentary on *Sūratu 'l- Ikhlāṣ* starts with some words on the method or *minhāj* it pursues, then passes on to the historical occasions that motivated its revelation and the world in which it was revealed. We will move from there to the other names by which Muslims have known it, then turn to its theme and subject matter by commenting on each verse. Next, we will enquire into the meaning of the letters that make up its words. Finally, we will look at the virtues of (*faḍā'il*) of *Sūratu 'l- Ikhlāṣ* and the spiritual rewards that attend its recitation.

Paul Hardy, PhD.

New York, NY

1

Subtleties of the Heart

The term used to describe commentary on the Qur'ān in Arabic is *"tafsīr"* derived from the three root letters *F-S-R*. They mean, "to explain," "to expound," "to explicate" or "to interpret." There are various methods of *tafsīr*. Generally, they correspond to the interests and aims of the author of the *tafsīr* called a *"mufassir"* and in the plural *"mufassirūn."* Each *tafsīr*, therefore, reflects a type of knowledge recognized among the Muslim religious sciences. In some, legal knowledge is the primary concern. In others, grammar holds precedence. In this *sūra* of course, no law is promulgated. There is no mention of what is permitted (*halāl*) or what is forbidden (*harām*). There is no talk even of Paradise or Hellfire. It mentions neither this world (*ad-dunyā*) nor the world to come (*al-ākhirah*). It touches only on Divine Realities, nothing else. That you might say limits the scope of its commentary beforehand and the type of knowledge it reflects.

When it comes to knowledge, the Prophet of Islam ﷺ placed it in two general categories. He said:

العلم علمان علم في القلب فذلك العلم النافع وعلم على اللسان فذلك حجة الله تعالى على ابن آدم

> Knowledge is of two kinds (*al-'ilmu 'ilmān):* there is knowledge of the heart (*'ilmu 'l-qalb*). That is the knowledge (*al-'ilmu'n-nāfi'*) that is of benefit. [Then] knowledge of the tongue (*'ilmu 'l-lisān*). The

latter is Allāh's proof for the child of Adam (*dhalika ḥujjatu 'l-Lāhi 'ala ibn adam*).[1]

Also, the Qur'ān speaks numerous times of those individuals who are "*ūlu 'l-albāb*," that is, "possessed of understanding hearts." Recall for example the famous verse at 3:190,

إِنَّ فِي خَلْقِ السَّمَاوَاتِ وَالأَرْضِ وَاخْتِلاَفِ اللَّيْلِ وَالنَّهَارِ لآيَاتٍ لِّأُوْلِي الأَلْبَابِ

"Surely, in the creation of the heavens and the earth are signs for those gifted with understanding hearts (*ūlu 'l-albāb*)."

Heart-knowledge (*'ilmu 'l-qalb*) has nothing to do with what heart means in today's language. Today, the word "heart" is term used to designate a figurative organ of sentiment, passion and feeling and has to do with the senses (*al-ḥawāss*). We see stylized pictures of the heart on St. Valentine's Day, calling to mind associations of romantic love. None of these things should be associated with the word "*qalb*" when we see it mentioned in the Qur'ān and Ḥadīth nor is it valid for the stations of the heart, "*fu'ād*" (pl. *af'idah*) or "*lubb*" (pl. *albāb*). The heart in these cases is always a super-sensuous organ. It is above the senses. Indeed it is beyond the intellect. It represents the core or the *lubb* of human reality. Of it the Prophet ﷺ said:

[1] A *mursal* tradition that al-Ḥākim narrated from al-Ḥasan and al-Khatīb from Jābir ﷺ.

إن قلوب بني ادم كلها بين إصبعين من أصابع الرحمن، كقلب واحد يصرفه
حيث يشاء، ثم قال رسول الله صلى الله عليه وسلم: اللهم مصرف
القلوب صرف قلوبنا على طاعتك

> The hearts of children of Adam are like a single heart between two of the fingers of the All Merciful. He turns it wherever He desires. O Allāh, Turner-of-hearts, turn our hearts toward obeying Thee.[2]

Heart-knowledge, therefore, is emphatically different from tongue knowledge (*ʿilmu 'l-lisān*).

The latter is, as the Prophet ﷺ indicated, knowledge that comes by proof (*ḥujjah*) or demonstration (*burhān*). After all, intellectual thought expresses itself in language and language is governed by rules of grammar (*an-naḥw*). Thought, on the other hand, is ideally governed by the rules of logic (*al-manṭiq*). Rules of grammar and logic imply a certain kind of constriction in what can be said or thought. In fact, the faculty of intellect is called in Arabic "*ʿaql*" from verb *ʿaqila* which means, "to fetter" as when one fetters or hobbles the forefeet of one's camel to keep it from roaming. The fetters are called "*ʿiqāl*." Hence, *ʿaql* conveys the idea of constriction in its root meaning. In using this term to describe the human function of reason, the Arab language wished to convey the innate limitation of reason.

In contrast to *ʿaql*, the heart or *qalb* has the root meaning of turning or revolving and thus conveys this organ's tremendous capacity

[2] Muslim's *Saḥīḥ*

for flexibility and transformation. This is why the heart can serve as the stage of Allāh's self-disclosures (*tajalīyyāt*) and outpourings (*fuyūḍāt*). Furthermore, we must remember "Every moment He (sc. Allāh) is on something new" (*kulla yawmin hūwa fī sha'n*) *as Sūratu 'r-Raḥmān* (55:29) tells us. That means that the time it takes to utter a sentence is still too long to catch what Allāh may wish to communicate to us.

Everything takes on the flavor of a particular situation so the telling about an event or happening is not the same as being there yourself. Even when you attempt to recount it, the meaning changes because the context of the recounting is different from the situation that saw the event's original occurrence. The people have changed and with the change of people so has the mood. The meaning has changed. For nothing remains the same in Allāh's creation from one moment to the next. As He, the Exalted says:

أَفَعَيِينَا بِالْخَلْقِ الْأَوَّلِ بَلْ هُمْ فِي لَبْسٍ مِّنْ خَلْقٍ جَدِيدٍ

"No indeed, but they are in confusion as to a new creation (*khalqin jadīd*)." (50:150)

There is then no repetition in the way Allāh discloses Himself, either in the Qur'ān or in the world at large. This is why Imām Abu 'l-Hasan al-Ashʿarī said: "The accident does not remain for two moments (*lā tabqā zamānayn*)." He meant the accidents (*aʿrāḍ*) of constant substances (*jawāhir*) that make up the universe.

The point here is that the heart is the only organ that is naturally adapted to the lack of repetition of divine disclosure. A often quoted ḥadīth *qudsī* or Divine Saying reported by the Prophet ﷺ, calls dramatic attention to the heart's great capacity for Divine expansiveness. It declares:

ما وسعني أرضي ولا سمائي ووسعني قلب عبدي المؤمن

> "My earth and My heaven encompasses Me not, but the heart of My believing servant doth encompass Me." [3]

Because of the heart's huge capacity and flexibility Allāh the Exalted can turn it as He wishes so that the Prophet ﷺ could pray and entreat his Lord," O Allāh, Turner of hearts, turn our hearts toward obeying Thee."

The lack of repetition in Divine Disclosure with respect to the Qur'ān means that the heart must attune itself to new meanings at every moment. Of course, this produces a different method from those used by grammarians, lawyers and ḥadīth experts when it comes to *tafsīr*. In contrast to those scholars, travelers on the path to Allāh, like Abū'l-'Abbās Ibn 'Aṭā', Abū 'Abdi-r-Raḥmān as-Sulamī, Abū 'l-Qāsim 'Abdu 'l-Karīm al-Qushayrī, have incorporated in their method (*minhāj*) of *tafsīr* the contents of *'ilmu 'l-qalb*.

For fourteen hundred years the scholars of the Muslim community (*'ulamā'u 'l-ummah*) the true and genuine *'ulamā'*, whose hearts Allāh has opened and given light with which to gaze upon realities of the Divine Kingdom, *malakūt*, have not ignored this data. For it is there, but not everyone can see it. Only those about whom Allāh has said:

[3] There are disputes over the authenticity or source of this tradition and some say it is an Isrā'īlī tradition. But there is an overwhelming truth to it according to the tradition narrated by aṭ-Ṭabarānī:

وآنية ربكم قلوب عباده الصالحين وأحبها إليه ألينها وأرقها

The receptacles of your Lord, are the hearts of His righteous servants, the most cherished, gentle and refined to Him.

أَلا إِنَّ أَوْلِيَاء اللّهِ لاَ خَوْفٌ عَلَيْهِمْ وَلاَ هُمْ يَحْزَنُونَ

"surely, for those who are Allāh's friend there is no fear nor cause to grieve (*inna awliyā'ul'Lāhi lā khawfan 'alayhim wa lā hum yaḥzanūn*)." (10:62)

can see it.

Given that Allāh Himself has conveyed such knowledge to such men and women in His holy book, how could any real scholar give an account of all the revelatory data deposited in the Qur'ān and Ḥadīth and ignore that sacred deposit?

Still, the inherent limitation of *'aql* has persuaded many scholars to explain away all the revelatory data that does not correspond to the rules governing reason. All the Islamic sciences operate at least at the level of reason. This is necessary because the capacity to reason things out step-by-step, is part of our natures created by Allāh. The latter is represented by ordinary linguistic expressions that suit our knowledge of the world of reason and perception. It is called the world of the visible, *'alam ash-shahādah,* because in the world of our most immediate environment we depend on step-step-reasoning and sense perception.

Knowledge about the world of *shahādah* to Muslim scholars is ideally the category called "*'ilmu 'l-'ibārah*" or "science of express meaning." Sciences that fall into this category have the task of explaining and expounding one thing in terms of another. The term *'ibārah* is a verbal noun formed from the Arabic verb *'abara* - "to cross, to traverse or to ford a stream" as when one crosses from one shore of an ocean to another. Crossing over is like speaking of one thing in terms of another. For shores insofar as they are limits to bodies of water, represent the same thing.

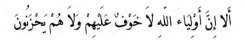

Accordingly, the Arabs speak of *"ta'bīru 'l-aḥlām"* or the interpretation of dreams because *ta'bīr* in the case of dreams makes it possible for one to go from the shore of the dream world , so to speak, to the shore of waking life. That is to say, dream interpretation makes it possible to pass from the images of the dream world to the realities of the waking world. For one interprets the events of a dream, for example, in terms of other events found in the course of everyday life. If it is a true dream, it is interpreted in terms of future events. But if the interpretation is to be illuminating and not more obscure than the dream itself the future events must be just like present events in kind and description, except they take place at a different time.

As said, every time you attempt to recount an event at which you were present to someone else, the meaning changes because the context of the recounting is different from the situation that saw the event's original occurrence. An example comes in the Qur'ān where its speaks of the Prophet Mūsā's (عليه السلام) glimpse of the fire of the burning bush from which Allāh was to speak to him. The verse from *Sūratu-l-Qaṣaṣ* reads:

فَلَمَّا قَضَى مُوسَى الْأَجَلَ وَسَارَ بِأَهْلِهِ آنَسَ مِن جَانِبِ
الطُّورِ نَارًا قَالَ لِأَهْلِهِ امْكُثُوا إِنِّي آنَسْتُ نَارًا لَّعَلِّي آتِيكُم
مِّنْهَا بِخَبَرٍ أَوْ جَذْوَةٍ مِّنَ النَّارِ لَعَلَّكُمْ تَصْطَلُونَ

Then, when Mūsā had fulfilled the term, and was traveling with his household, he saw in the distance a fire and said unto his household: Bide ye [here]. Lo! I see in the distance a fire: peradventure I shall bring you a report (*khabar*) from there, or a

brand from the fire that ye may warm yourselves.
(28:29)

The Prophet Mūsā ﷺ exclaims, "'Lo! I see in the distance a fire' and said," according to the Qur'ān "to his people, 'perhaps I shall bring you a report (khabar) from there or a brand from the fire that you may warm yourselves.'"

In the Qur'ān's recounting of Mūsā's sighting of the fire of the burning bush, the locus of the divine voice sighting in the distance, Imām al-Ghazālī finds a distinction between two types of knowledge. The Qur'ān alludes to the knowledge possessed by the people who warm themselves by the lighted firebrand and that owned by the people who hear the report. The people who warm themselves with the fire experience a tasting (dhawq) of the fire of the burning bush from which Allāh spoke. " Imām al-Ghazālī says, "Only a person who has a fiery brand—that is the fire of a light-giving lamp (*sirājan munīra*) of the prophetic spirit can warm himself, not the one who hears a report (khabar) about fire." The latter are without tasting; they merely follow what it says by rote (*taqlīd*). They only hear a report or *khabar*. These are the *ʿulamā'u 'l-ʿibārah*.

Dhawq - tasting, therefore differs from knowledge, *ʿilm*. It is thus possible to see the distinction between these two levels of knowledge as rooted in the two verbs used to express the act of knowing in Arabic — *ʿalima* and *ʿarifa*. "*ʿIlm*" derived from a transitive root *ʿ-L-M* (ع ل م) and may take two objects (*yataʿaddī ilā mafʿūlayn*)—"to know someone as someone or something." For example, one may say "I know Zayd as standing" (*ʿalimtu zaydan qā'iman*).

But *maʿrifah* is derived from an intransitive root (*ʿ-R-F* - ع ر ف) that takes only one object. Yet, when the Arab grammarians say that *ʿ-L-M* because it takes two objects, the relation between Zayd and the act of standing (*al-qiyām*) is identical with the knowledge of Zayd and standing, they miss an important point. In fact, both Zayd and his standing must have been known before a relationship between them could have been known. Thus, *maʿrifah* has to come before *ʿilm.*

At the same time, because *maʿrifah* takes only one object it describes perfectly the nature of cognition experienced in *dhawq*. Neither *maʿrifah* nor *dhawq*, then, are reducible to *ʿilmu 'l-ʿibārah. Dhawq* is non-linguistic in character. Thus, it has no repeatable content. In this way it is like its physical analogue. For each time we taste a thing it is subtly different, even if it is a bite from the same piece of fruit. When we write something down, however, the words and sentences we use can be repeated over and over again. Thus, one of the travelers (*sālikūn*) on the path to God in was heard to recite in *al-Madīnātu 'l-Munawwarah* some years ago:

ʿindanā ʿilmu wajdāni wa-adhwāq

We own a knowledge of tasting and finding,

lā yu'khadhu mini 'l-kutubi wa 'l-awrāq

not taken from papers and books

ʿilmunā laysa bi 'l-qīla wa 'l-qāla

The knowledge we have is not "he said" and "she said,"

wa-lakinna bi-khidmati fuḥūli 'r-rijāl.

But comes through the service of illustrious men.

Dhawq is used to describe the non-repeatable events of Divine Self-disclosures (*tajallīyāt*). To express cognition of unrepeatable Divine Disclosures in the Qur'ān, the *mufassirūn* follow the method of *ishārah*. The latter literally means "to point." As Shaykh ʿAbdū 'l-Ghanī an-Nāblusī explains, one can by pointing signify all at once (*dafʿtan*) things it would need many words to express (*ʿabara*) verbally (*bi 'l-lafẓ*). One thus alludes to things that are not said expressly. For Allāh in the Qur'ān may say one thing and simultaneously allude to another. Accordingly, Imām ʿAbdu 'l-Karīm al-Qushayrī called his *tafsīr* on the Qur'ān, *Laṭā'ifu 'l-Ishārāt* or *The Subtleties of Allusive Meanings.* He could just as well have called it the "Subtleties of the Heart" since it contains the intimation of Allāh to His servants, the *ʿārifūn' bi 'l-Lāh*—those who know on the strength of what Allāh teaches them.

The *ʿārifūn' bi 'l-Lāh* or *Āhlu-dh-Dhawq*—The People Capable of Tasting, naturally favor this method of *tafsīr* since their kind of knowledge does not fit into the category of *ʿilmu 'l-ʿibārah*—knowledge of law (*fiqh*), grammar, etc. Rather, it is the same kind of knowledge that Allāh taught to the prophet Mūsā ﷺ at the hands of Khiḍr; for in *Sūratu 'l-Kahf* we read,

وَعَلَّمْنَاهُ مِن لَّدُنَّا عِلْمًا

Wa ʿallamnāhu min ladunna ʿilman
"We had taught him knowledge from out presence" (*Sūratu-l-Kahf*, 18:65)

That is, Allāh taught him what the scholars of Islam call "*ʿilmun ladunnī.*" It is only possessed by the *ʿarif bi 'l-Lāh* —the one whom Allāh Himself has taught.

In the schools of Islam, this is highest knowledge taught, but it cannot be learned from books. Muslim theologians affirm that their science, — *ʿilmu 'l-kalām* —"the science of discourse about Allāh"—is in fact cancelled out by the truth of *maʿrifah*. For the *ʿarif bi 'l-Lāh* knows all things only through Allāh, not from reading papers (*awrāq*). He knows from tasting (*adhwāq*). Someone who has experienced that level of knowledge then teaches not by books but in sessions of live associations. That is why the *sālik* quoted earlier said: "The knowledge we have is not 'he said' and 'she said'/ but comes through the service of illustrious men (*ʿilmunā laysa bi 'l-qīla wa 'l-qāla/ wa-lakinna bi-khidmati fuḥūli'r-*

rijāl)." The service comes in association or what is called in Arabic "*suḥba.*"

In fact, the commentary that follows arises from such associations among those traveling (*sālikūn*) the path to Allāh and passed down from masters—especially the masters belonging to the "Golden Chain" (*as-Silsalatu 'dh-Dhāhabīyya*) of spiritual authority in Islam. This Golden Chain began with the Prophet ﷺ who said:

ما صب الله في صدري شيئا إلا وصببته في صدر أبي بكر

> "What Allāh hath poured into my heart I have poured in the heart of Abū Bakr aṣ-Ṣiddīq."[4]

From Abū Bakr, this precious spiritual heritage passed to Shāh Bahā'ud-Dīn Naqshband. In our own day it has come to Grand Shaykh 'Abd Allāh ad-Daghestānī and then to Mawlāna Shaykh Muḥammad Naẓim al-Ḥaqqānī.

Today, there are people who question that high authority. They say, "How do these men and women know these realities and we are unable to know them; how did they bring them that up, and how can they consider that such knowledge exists of things we cannot see?" These critics restrict their knowledge to what they can represent in their minds as sense data or reasoning based on such data. Thus, they conceived the meanings manifest in the Qur'ān in the narrowest way possible. So what the world turns out to be is different from what those narrow-minded people think.

Contemporary science has shown time again and again that the actual world reveals itself to be quantum mechanical, or quantum field theoretic or quantum string theoretic as an earlier writing, *The Approach of Armageddon,* explained. Take any object then.

[4] *Nuzhaṭ al-Majālis.*

Break it down into its constituent components. You will find it is made of different subatomic particles that come together and form that. Science is looking at the smallest possible elements from which things known to our faculties as objects, such as a table or chair, are made. This is not to deny that there are sense-objects extended in space and time like tables and chairs. But the idea is that all the facts about objects like that are determined, in principle, by the facts about the particles of which they are composed.

Still, knowledge of contemporary science corresponds only to the world of God's sovereignty, dominion and testimony, that is, His *mulk w'ash-shahādah.* It is also called the realm of *Nasūt* or the human realm. It is world of bodily forms, for man is created from earth and the "world of sensation" (*'alam al-ḥiss*). Everyone who walks on the earth walks in the world of *mulk,* Imām al-Ghazālī says [5]in his *Iḥya' 'ulūmi'd'Dīn* (*Revival of the Religious Sciences).* Yet, beyond the world of *mulk,* there is the world of power or *jabarūt* and the world of royalty or *malakūt.* And even beyond those worlds, are the worlds of *Lāhūt* and *Hāhūt,* from "*hūwa*" the second word of *Sūratu 'l-Ikhlāṣ.* So the world that turns out to be in actuality real is vastly different from the world as it appears to the naked eye and the other four senses. What is more, in comparison to these other worlds, the dominion of *mulk* is like a ring cast in the desert.

Still, there is a continuity of vision between the physical realm and that of the spiritual. In *Mishkāt al-anwār* Imām al-Ghazālī observes how *al-mulk w'ash-shahādah* "parallel[s] the world of *malakūt.*"

[5] Imām al-Ghazālī, *Iḥyā'u 'l-'ulūmi 'd-dīn* (*Revival of the Religious Sciences),* (chapter *Kitāb at-tawḥīd wa 't-tawakkul* (Book of Divine Oneness and trusting in God).

Moreover, that "there is nothing in the former that is not a representation (*mithāl*) for something in the latter." As Allāh says in *Sūratu 'l-Mulk*:

مَّا تَرَى فِي خَلْقِ الرَّحْمَنِ مِن تَفَاوُتٍ فَارْجِعِ الْبَصَرَ هَلْ تَرَى مِن فُطُورٍ

mā tara fī khalqi 'r-Raḥmāni min tafāwut f'arji'i 'l-baṣara hal tarā min fuṭūr

"There is no fault line in the creation of the All-Merciful. So look again! Do you see a rift?" (67:2-3)

Thus, for example, both the *'ārif bi 'l-Lāh* and scientists look upon a universe as originating ultimately in intense energy in the form of light, as we showed in *The Approach of Armageddon*.

Nevertheless, the world of *mulk* contrasts with the worlds of *jabarūt* and *malakūt* which the *'arif bi 'l-Lāh* beholds. In those latter realms, things do not have the fixity we associate with rocks, chairs, tables, mountains, etc. Rather, reality moves rapidly, shifting from moment to moment. Each single moment brings a new order of being on whose face is written an entirely new meaning. As Allāh declares in *Sūratu 'r-Raḥmān*:

كُلَّ يَوْمٍ هُوَ فِي شَأْنٍ

kulla yawmin hūwa fī shā'n

"Every moment He (i.e., Allāh) is on some new task." (55:29)

The realities of *jabarūt* and *malakūt* displayed from behind the veil of *mulk* are thus seen to fluctuate and become different at every instant through a wide variety of possible meanings. Every moment brings something new.

Hence, it is impossible for a meaning to remain fixed long enough to attach a predicate (*khabar*) to a subject (*mubtadi'*) to form a sentence (*jumlah*). A thing's significance has changed even before the predicate is thought or uttered. One has no time to formulate an argument (*ḥujjah*) or demonstration (*burhān*).

Intellect or *'aql* then is at a disadvantage in uncovering such meanings. Its very job is to fetter and tie down meaning in sentences that make up arguments and demonstration. But Imām al-Ghazālī says in *Kitāb 'Ajā'ib'u 'l-qalb* (*The Book of the Wonders of the Heart*) from the *Iḥyā'ul-'ulūmi'd-dīn* (*The Revivication of the Sciences of the Faith*):

تعالى فيلمع في القلوب من وراء ستر الغيب شيء من غرائب العلم تارة كالبرق الخاطف

"There is a flash in hearts from behind the curtain of the invisible realm (*al-ghayb*) ...like the sudden flash of lightning (*al-barqu 'l-khāṭif*)."

So by the time one has spoken or written even a sentence, that flash has vanished and some new reality has taken its place. Hence, what the Prophet called *'ilmu 'l-lisān* —knowledge of the tongue, is too slow. Only the heart quickly turning can capture that reality. In the same understanding, Imām al-Ghazālī places these flashings in the category of inspiration or "*ilhām*."

"Express knowledge" or *'ilmu 'l-'ibārah* is also inadequate because it is always indirect and has not the immediacy of "tasting" (*dhawq*). For you cannot taste what I have tasted. Yet, I can point to my tasting or teach it to you by allusion, that is, by *ishārah*.

Given that Allāh Himself has conveyed heart-knowledge in His holy book, how else could any real scholar give an account of all the revelatory data posited in the Qur'ān and Ḥadīth and leave out the results coming from this noble method? And to those who find difficulty with that, we offer the advice of Imām al-Ghazālī who said:

> Knowledge (*ʿilm*) is above faith and tasting (*dhawq*) is above knowledge. For tasting is finding (*wajdān*), but knowing is seeing one thing in terms of another, and having faith is a mere acceptance through rote imitation (*taqlīd*). Therefore, have a good opinion of the people of finding and gnosis (*ʿirfān*).

The approach here then does not ignore results *ʿilmu ʾl-ʿibārah* with respect to grammar and ḥadīth. But it will include the results of *ʿilmu ʾl-ishārah* insofar as these show themselves to be apposite.

2

Why Was Sūratu 'l-Ikhlāṣ Revealed?

The reasons behind the revelation (*asbābu'n-nuzūl*) of *Sūratu 'l-Ikhlāṣ* are given in a number of ḥadīths. These traditions show that different people on different occasions questioned the Holy Prophet ﷺ about the Essence and Nature of the God to Whose service and worship he invited them. On each different occasion, he recited this very *sūrah* in response. First, the pagans of his own family, the Quraysh, asked him this question in Mecca. In reply this *sūrah* was sent. Then the Jews and the Christians asked him a similar question. Again, it is reported that the same words were revealed. The fact Allāh revealed the same words to answer these different questions at various times should not leave us with the impression that these Ḥadīth are in any way at odds with one another. Nor should we think that they are untrue to historical fact. Often, Allāh inspired the Prophet ﷺ to recite apparently identical words on different occasions.

We must keep in mind that the meaning of the words in the various *sūras* of the Qur'ān shifts along with their context of revelation. For Allāh says, *kulla yawmin hūwa fī sha'n*" — "Every moment He is on something new." Hence, the same verses can appear with a different significance depending upon the context of their revelation. This is why Imām al-Qushayrī in his famous *tafsīr* on the Qur'ān, *Laṭā'ifu 'l-Ishārāt* (*The Subtleties of Allusive Meanings*) gives a different commentary to the words *bismi'l-Lāhi 'r-Raḥmāni 'r-Raḥīm* — "In the name of the All-Merciful, the Compassionate" — that begins every *sūrah* except one in the Qur'ān. Each time the *bismil-Lāhi 'r-Raḥmāni 'r-Raḥīm* used it has a different significance according to the context in which the *sūrah* was revealed. It's meaning, in other words, changes to fit the occasion.

The situation is the same for each time *Sūratu 'l-I<u>kh</u>lāṣ* is mentioned as being revealed. Each time it has a different significance depending on the occasion. It does not mean that one report is true and the others false. No! All the reports are true and have historical value. We start then with Daḥḥāk's report:

ال الضحاك: إن المشركين أرسلوا عامر بن الطفيل إلى النبي صلى الله عليه وسلم وقالوا: شققت عصانا وسببت آلهتنا، وخالفت دين آبائك، فإن كنت فقيراً أغنيناك، وإن كنت مجنوناً داويناك، وإن هويت امرأة زوجناكها، فقال عليه الصلاة والسلام: " لست بفقير، ولا مجنون، ولا هويت امرأة، أنا رسول الله أدعوكم من عبادة الأصنام إلى عبادته، " فأرسلوه ثانية وقالوا :قل له بين لنا جنس معبودك، أمن ذهب أو فضة، فأنزل الله هذه السورة، فقالوا له: ثلثمائة وستون صنماً لا تقوم بحوائجنا، فكيف يقوم الواحد بحوائج الخلق؟ فنزلت: ﴿ وَلصَّٰٓفَّٰتِ ﴾ إلى قوله: } إِنَّ إِلَٰهَكُمْ لَوَاحِدٌ] {الصافات: 1–4] فأرسلوه أخرى، وقالوا: بين لنا أفعاله فنزل } إِنَّ رَبَّكُمُ للَّهُ لَّذِى خَلَقَ لسَّمَٰوَاتِ وَلأَرْضِ{

The idolaters sent ʿAmir ibnu 'ṭ-Ṭufayl with a message to the Prophet ﷺ, saying, "You have broken ranks with our community (*<u>sh</u>aqaqta ʿasāna*), provoked our divinities and abandoned the religion of your forefathers. If you are poor, we will give you money you. If you suffer mental affliction, your madness we will treat. If it is a woman whom you desire, we will marry you to her." The Prophet ﷺ replied: "I am neither poor nor mad. Nor do I desire a woman. I am the Messenger of Allāh who has summoned you [to abandon] your worship of idols [and] invited you to worship the One God, Allāh. Then they sent unto him a second message and said, "Say to him: 'Make clear to us the kind (*jins*) of object you worship (*maʿbūdak).* Is it made of gold or of silver?" Then did Allāh revealed this *sūra*, "*Qul! Hūwa Allāh Āḥad.*" Then they said to him, "Three hundred and sixty idols do not accomplish our needs, how in the world will but one (*al-wāḥid*) accomplish the needs of the people?" Then Allāh revealed, "By the Angels Standing in ranks... Of a surety, is your divinity indeed One (*inna ilāhakum la-wāḥid*)." (37:4) Then did the idolaters send unto him yet another message and said, "Explain to us what is it that your God does?" Then was revealed the verse, "Surely, your Lord is Allāh who had created the heavens and the earth."[6]

In other narrations, it is reported that the idolaters among the Arabs (*mushrikū'l-ʿarab*) asked of the Prophet ﷺ,

صف لنا ربك ما هو؟ ومن أي شيء هو؟ فأنزل الله ﴿قل هو الله أحد الله الصمد لم يلد ولم يولد ولم يكن له كفوا أحد﴾

[6] Al-Rāzī in his *Mafātīḥ*.

> "O Messenger of Allāh! Describe to us your Lord what He is (*ṣif lanā rabbaka mā hūwa*)."[7]

That is, give us your Lord's attributes. It was then that Allāh sent down the words, *"Qul! Hūwa Allāhu Āḥad…"*

We find other traditions relating to the circumstances of the *sūra's* revelation. One ḥadīth transmitted by 'Ikrimah on the authority of Ibn 'Abbās relates that:

> حدثنا ابن حميد، قال: ثنا سلمة، قال: ثني ابن إسحاق، عن محمد، عن سعيد، قال: أتى رهط من اليهود نبي الله صلى الله عليه وسلم، فقالوا: يا محمد، هذا الله خلق الخلق، فمن خلقه؟ فغضب النبي صلى الله عليه وسلم حتى انتقع لونه، ثم ساورهم غضبا لربه؛ فجاءه جبريل فسكنه، وقال: اخفض عليك جناحك يا محمد، وجاءه من الله جواب ما سألوه عنه، قال: يقول الله تبارك وتعالى: ﴿قل هو الله أحد الله الصمد لم يلد ولم يولد ولم يكن له كفو أحد﴾ فلما تلاها عليهم النبي صلى الله عليه وسلم قالوا: صف لنا ربك؛ كيف خلقه، وكيف عضده، وكيف ذراعه؟ فغضب النبي صلى الله عليه وسلم أشد من غضبه الأول، ثم ساورهم، فأتاه جبريل فقال مثل مقالته، وأتاه بجواب ما

[7] Ibn Jarīr reported it from 'Ikrimah ﷺ.

سألوه عنه ﴿وما قدروا الله حق قدره والأرض جميعا قبضته يوم القيامة والسموات مطويات بيمينه سبحانه وتعالى عما يشركون

The Jews came to the Messenger of Allāh ﷺ along with Kaʿb ibnu 'l-Aʿraf. They said, "O Muḥammad! This Allāh fashioned creation. But who created Allāh?" The Prophet ﷺ of Allāh became angry. Jibrīl descended and calmed him[, saying,] "O Muḥammad! lower thy wings!" Then "*Qul! Hūwa Allāh Āḥad...*" was revealed. The Prophet ﷺ proceeded to read it to them.

After the Messenger had recited it to them, they said, "Describe to us your Lord: What is His nature? And how is His fingers? And how is His arm?

The Prophet of Allāh ﷺ became angrier than the previous time. Jibrīl descended and calmed him with what he had said before and came to him with the answer to what they had asked, saying: "No just estimate have they made of Allāh, such as is due to Him: On the Day of Judgment the whole of the earth will be but His handful, and the heavens will be rolled up in His right hand: Glory to Him! High is He above the Partners they attribute to Him!" (Sūratu 'z-Zumar, 39:67)

And in another version:

The Jews then said, "What power, what strength hath He in his forearm?" Thereupon the Prophet became yet angrier and Jibrīl brought the verse,

> "They measured not the power of Allāh [according to] its true measure when they said, "Allāh hath revealed naught to a human being. Say! Who sent down the Book that Moses brought as light and a guidance to humankind? You put into parchments, revealing much therein and hiding much. Yet, you were taught that which you knew not, both you and your forefathers." (6:91; cf. 39:67)[8]

That is, the same God who revealed Torah is now sending down the Qur'ān. But this was a fact the Jewish People of the Book were slow to admit. They came to the Prophet to test him in order to decide the truth of the matter for themselves. In a sense their behavior was to be expected. The Jews, after all, saw themselves as the custodians of monotheism in that region and thus scrupulously guarded the faith that they inherited to the best of their ability.

Nevertheless, the revelation of *Sūratu 'l-Ikhlāṣ* appeared as something entirely new to the horizon of the ancient Jewish world. Monotheism became manifest in an unexpected way. With this development, it was no longer to be the preserve of one people or tribe but open to all humankind. Allāh in His supreme mystery always has surprises, even for those whom He holds close and loves. Another version of the ḥadīth also highlights the scrupulosity of the Jewish people of the Book in guarding their faith. It is related by Qatāda, ad-Daḥḥāk and Muqātil and al-Wāḥidī quotes it in his *Asbābu'n-Nuzūli 'l-Qur'ān*:

[8] This tradition is recorded by Ibn Jarīr and ibn al-Mundhir from Saʿīd bin Jubayr ﷺ.

لما قالوا لرسول الله صلى: صف لنا ربك، أمن ذهب هو أم من نحاس

أم من صفر؟ فقال الله عز وجل ردا عليهم: "قل هو والله أحد" ففي

"هو" دلالة على موضع الرد، ومكان الجواب

People from the Jews came to the Prophet ﷺ saying, "Describe to us your Lord! For Allāh described His attribute (*na't*) to us in revealing Torah. Narrate to us of which thing is he (*hūwa*)? Of what sort (*jins*) of thing is He? Is He made of gold or brass, or silver. From whom does he inherit the world (*dunya*)? And who will inherit it from him?" Thereupon, Allāh revealed this *sūrah* to give a description of His attributes in a special fashion.[9]

عن أنس رضي الله عنه قال: جاءت يهود خيبر إلى النبي صلى الله عليه

وسلم فقالوا: يا أبا القاسم خلق الله الملائكة من نور الحجاب وآدم من

حمأ مسنون وإبليس من لهب النار، والسماء من دخان، والأرض من

زبد الماء، فأخبرنا عن ربك فلم يجبهم النبي صلى الله عليه وسلم، فأتاه

جبريل بهذه السورة ﴿قل هو الله أحد﴾

Again, a report has come that the Jewish People of the Book in Khaybar approached the Prophet ﷺ and said, "O Abū 'l-Qāsim! Allāh created the

[9] Al-Qurṭubī cites this in his tafsīr on the proof of the authority of the masters of commentary.

> angels from the light of the Veil and Adam from the fetid miry clay, Iblīs from the flame of fire and the heavens from the smoke and the earth from the foam of water, so tell us about your Lord. The Prophet ﷺ gave them no reply. Then Jibrīl brought to him this *sūrah*, "*Qul! Hūwa Allāh Āḥad...*" [10]

Note how the Prophet ﷺ held back from answering them and waited upon the divine revelation (*waḥīy*). He behaved in this way even though he already knew the answer. Had not Allāh given him knowledge of the first and the last (*'ulūm al-awwalīn wa 'l-ākhirīn*)? Still, he would not answer until the answer came to him. In this incident, there is a moral.

People often claim to have knowledge, even when they, in fact, do not know. They do this to avoid appearing ignorant. But note the Prophet's ﷺ behavior. His behavior reveals to us the correct way to act in such occasions. He waited. Then Jibrīl ﷺ brought this *Sūratu 'l-Ikhlāṣ*.

Finally, in yet another ḥadīth we find a report that the Christians came to the Prophet ﷺ. That is, 'Aṭā transmits on the authority of Ibn 'Abbās ﷺ that:

روى عطاء عن ابن عباس، قال: قدم وفد نجران، فقالوا: صف لنا ربك
أمن زبرجد أو ياقوت، أو ذهب، أو فضة؟ فقال: " إن ربي ليس من
شيء لأنه خالق الأشياء " فنزلت: ﴿ قُلْ هُوَ ٱللَّهُ أَحَدٌ ﴾ قالوا: هو
واحد، وأنت واحد، فقال: ليس كمثله شيء، قالوا: زدنا من الصفة،

[10] Recorded from Ibn Jarīr on the authority of Abū al-'Alīyyah ﷺ.

فقال: ﴿ ٱللَّهُ ٱلصَّمَدُ ﴾ فقالوا: وما الصمد؟ فقال: الذي يصمد إليه الخلق في الحوائج، فقالوا: زدنا فنزل: ﴿ لَمْ يَلِدْ ﴾ كما ولدت مريم: ﴿ وَلَمْ يُولَدْ ﴾ كما ولد عيسى: ﴿ وَلَمْ يَكُن لَّهُۥ كُفُوًا أَحَدٌۢ ﴾ يريد نظيراً من خلقه

A delegation from Najrān arrived. They said, "Describe to us your Lord! Is He made of chrysolite or corundum, gold or silver?" The Prophet ﷺ replied, "He is not made of anything. He is the Creator of all things." Thereupon, was revealed "*Qul! Hūwa Allāh Āḥad...*" The Christians said, "He is one (*wāḥidun*) and you are one (*wāḥidun*)." The Prophet ﷺ answered, "Nothing is like Him. (*laysa ka-mithlihi shay'un*). Then they said: "Add to your description!" The Prophet ﷺ continued and said, "He is *ṣamaḍ*." They asked: "What is *ṣamaḍ*?" The Prophet ﷺ answered, "He is the One whom creatures approach when in need." Then the Christians said, "Tell us more!" Thereupon was revealed, "He does not beget" like Maryam begot. "He is not born" just as ʿĪsa was begotten. "Equal to Him is not any one." It means none of His creatures is equal to Him.[11]

In another narration the Christians say, "O Muḥammad, tell us what is your Lord like and of what substance is He made?" The Prophet ﷺ

[11] *Ibid.*

> replied, "My Lord is not made from any substance. He is Unique and Exalted above everything."

Thereupon Allāh sent down this remarkable *sūra*. It is remarkable first because humankind had for so long awaited its message. Of course, monotheism versus polytheism in the Near East had long been a matter of debate.

But going back over these *aḥādīth* giving the reasons why *Sūratu 'l-Ikhlāṣ* was revealed, it is noteworthy that each of three groups who approached the Prophet ﷺ represent parties to the debate over the oneness of God as it had emerged up to that time. First, there are the polytheists. Now it is true that in these *aḥādīth* the polytheists portrayed are Arabs. However, it would be wrong to think that they merely represent the situation of polytheism among the Arabs. Rather, they symbolize the general situation of polytheism as it had existed for centuries in the world.

3

The World in which Sūratu 'l-Ikhlāṣ Was Revealed

In the world in which *Sūratu 'l-Ikhlāṣ* was revealed. Monotheism was the exception rather than the rule. Polytheism is generally characterized by the fact the names of divinities amount to no more than descriptions of powers found in nature. Such powers display themselves in the same way for all the world's inhabitants. The sun and moon rise and set for everyone, for example, everyone walks on the face of the earth; all people look up and see the sky. The heavens send down rain and the earth sends up plants and trees everywhere.

But that means that the powers worshipped in one place and by one people are easily translatable into those worshiped in another place by other people. Translatability was made easy in the Greek language, for example, because the term for God - *theos* - is not a proper name. The same is true for the term *"deus"* in Latin. Rather, these terms are descriptive terms that stand in for predicates in sentences, not subjects. Polytheists, in other words, were so impressed or awed by natural powers that they said "this is a god" or "that is a god." Any power or force at work in the world that outlasts human beings could for this reason be called a god. Hence, the debate between polytheism and monotheism took on a semantic dimension. That is, Divine Names not only enable us to refer to something; they mean something as well. Or rather, such names refer to something by describing it.

So before the revelation of the Qur'ān in Arabia and elsewhere, the meaning of a Divine Name unfolded itself in myths (*asāṭir*) and rites, etc. Those myths and rites give names describing the powers of deities in terns of various functions found in nature. Depicted in these terms, one deity becomes easily comparable to other ones with similar traits. It makes no difference whether they are Greek, Roman, Egyptian, or Arab. Their similarity insofar as they describe the powers of nature makes their names mutually translatable. The sun god of one religion was easily equated with the sun god of another religion. It is this framework prevalent among all polytheists that makes it appropriate that we should take the *mushriku 'l-'arab* as representing all idolaters since the beginning of time.

Now when the Christians took over the Greek and Latin languages they also took over the capacity of "*theos*" and "*deus*" to signify more than one god. "*Theos*" and "*deus*" can signify several divinities at the same time. It was this fact that allowed the Christians to say that God signifies three Divine Realities and one at the same time. It also means that the Christian missionary and the polytheist can use the word "God" in the same sense. So when the idolater says his idol is God and when the missionary says that the polytheist's idol is not God, but only a senseless block of wood, they have no disagreement about the meaning of the word "God."

Thus, "*Deus*" translates "*Theos*" and "God" translates "*Deus*." A proper name, in contrast, is like Zayd or Hind. When proper names are carried over into other languages, they require transliteration, not translation. This is what happens in the case of "Allāh" which, when found in English texts, Latin letters represent the originally Arabic Divine Name.

The way the Jews phrased their question to Prophet ﷺ illustrates the general understanding that the names people used for the Divine have a general and not particular significance. They did not ask for the proper name of Muḥammad's Lord. They asked, "Of what kind (*jins*) of thing is your Lord?" Or more literally, "What genus is your Lord? Now "*jins*" is not originally an Arabic word. It is a translation or rather transliteration. Languages spoken by Muslims like Persian and Urdu sometimes use the Farsi Divine Name "*khoda*" in place of Allāh. But remember that users of those languages are also familiar with the name "Allāh." They pray in Arabic and write their languages using of the Greek word "*genos*" which in Latin becomes "*genus*."

English speakers took over the Latin word directly. "Genus," as any biologist or logician will tell us, applies to more than one thing. The formulators of the doctrine of the trinity found this important. It meant that when three things are united by genus, they could be multiple and one at the same time. This is called unity of "*genus*." Generic unity is illustrated by the genus called "animal." "Animal" unites under a single idea horse, man, and dog. The members of the trinity are one in their genus, godhood.

Be this as it may, the God of Israel had come to be seen by non-Jews and even Jews themselves as inseparably linked to one people, the nation of the Hebrews. This is why the Qur'ān had to remind them that Allāh to whose worship Muḥammad ﷺ called them was none other than the God of Moses ﵇. In consequence, Allāh commanded the Prophet ﷺ to ask the Jews:

أَنزَلَ الْكِتَابَ الَّذِي جَاءَ بِهِ مُوسَىٰ نُورًا وَهُدًى لِّلنَّاسِ

"Who sent down the Book that Moses brought as light and a guidance to humankind." (7:91)

And so it is throughout the Qur'ān where the Jews are being constantly reminded of their failure to adhere to the Divine Will by calling humankind to worship one Lord. In sum, the polytheistic climate that prevailed throughout the world in the days leading up to Islam made cultural diversity possible. One could worship whatever god or have any religion one liked. It only had to be a religion and a worship of identifiable gods that were, in principle contactable by all. That is, they had to be the very same gods only worshipped under different names.

The powerful influence of this way of thinking can be seen in its effect upon the international trade relations of the ancient Middle East. Consider, for an example, the practice of swearing oaths. It originated in the social need to ratify pacts and agreements. Ratification could take many forms. One form, the handshake continues in the Middle East until this day. In fact, the use o f the word "*yamīn*" (right hand) to mean "oath" originated in this practice. But ratification also took place in the presence of witnesses, the most important of whom naturally were the gods themselves. But these gods could not be ones known only by one party to a treaty and not the other. For a treaty or contract to be properly sealed, they had to be witnessed by divinities known and recognized by all the parties concerned.

Moreover, all divinities called upon to stand as witnesses had to be of the same rank and function. This is the background of oath swearing in the Qur'ān. The letter *wāw, tā'* or *bā'* are all used to signify the swearing of the oath (*al-qasam*). For example, we read in the second verse of *Sūratu 'z-Zukhruf*:

أَمْ آتَيْنَاهُمْ كِتَابًا مِّن قَبْلِهِ فَهُم بِهِ مُسْتَمْسِكُونَ

wa 'l-kitābu 'l-mubīn

"By the Book (i.e., the Qur'ān) which maketh plain"

(43:21)

where Allāh swears by His own word. This verse begins with the letter *wāw*, called *Wāwu 'l-qasam*, the most frequent form of oath in Qur'an obviously denotes accompaniment (*ma'īyah*) the joining of one thing to another (*ḍammu 'sh-shay'i bi 'sh-shay'*). Hence, in swearing an oath by a person or a thing, one wishes that person or thing to "bear him company" or "stand by him."

The principal function of the oath is to provide a *dalīl* or evidence, a *shahādah* or a testimony. In swearing an oath by a certain divinity, one presents that divinity as evidence supporting one's statement. One, in other words, stakes the god's honor on the contract made. So, the gods the parties invoke ought to be easily recognized by all partners to the contract, if not in name, at least, in function and power. However, the Qur'ān is Allāh's very word. And Allāh does not need to stake His honor on anything. He does not need to cite anyone or anything in support of what He says, since He is the Creator of all things.

Thus, for ancient polytheists never far from the socio-economic realities of everyday life, monotheism was highly problematic. If international trade and law depended on the translatability of one's regional and cultural god into that of someone else's regional and cultural god, what was to be done in dealing with those who worshipped a God who transcended all functional equivalents and whose name was furthermore untranslatable? For the name "Allāh" is a proper name. It may be *transliterated* but not translated, since there is no god that is His equivalent, neither in function nor in power.

Given the role their divinities played in commercial life of the Arabs, it seemed to the idolaters of the Arabs that the Prophet's invitation to worship Allāh, the Unique was economically motivated. That is why the Quraysh asked Muḥammad ﷺ if he were poor and in economic need. If the above ḥadīths tell us anything, they communicate a living picture of ancient polytheism, a picture different from any we otherwise might have imagined. Islam arrived on a theological scene where the shapes and names of gods might have differed vastly. But their functions over large areas of the ancient world remained remarkably the same. They represented the natural functions of growth and fertility, the social functions of warfare and commerce, etc. That explains why each group put their God on the same level with respect to truth.

Indeed, prior to the advent of Islam, the question of truth or falsity in religion had not yet arisen in the Arabian Peninsula. Indeed, truth had not ever been an issue where religion was concerned. Or rather, it had not emerged in any truly effective fashion. The religion of the Arab idolaters before Muḥammad ﷺ did not automatically call everything outside itself into a position of error and falsehood. In fact, truth and falsehood were, never at issue in ancient polytheism. Religion was a relative matter and divinity reducible simply to the relations in which people-stood to their gods.

These different relations unfolded in a series of different myths and rites that told the stories of the natural powers of the universe. There were myths and rites fashioned to glorify solar power, for example. For each group had its sun god just as each had its god and goddesses of reproduction, of death, and of life. The names of these gods varied. Their functions, however, remained ever the same. In this situation, no one true god emerged, no one true mode of worship, no one true religion to bind the human conscience. Even if the Jews in the time of the Prophet ﷺ had objected to this relativism, their objection would have had little effect.

Long before the advent of Islam, Judaism had virtually become a tribal religion. At least, it appeared as such in the Arabian Peninsula in the seventh century of the Common Era. For this reason, the idolaters saw the Jewish God as little different from their own. The Arabs had their many gods. The Jews had their one God. Judaism then was not an effective barrier to the relativism in theological matters that prevailed throughout the Middle East at this time.

But neither was Christianity. Its adoption of a doctrine of relative unity was mentioned earlier. At least for two hundred or more years prior to Islam Christians had been arguing that three things are one in same godhood on the analogy of the unity of several species of things in the same "genus." Having taken this step, they went further and introduced relativity into the very essence of Divinity itself. They named God the Father and the Prophet Jesus God's son. So, the Divine Name "Father" brought with it the relation of fatherhood and the Divine Name "Son" brought with it the relation of sonship. Fatherhood describes the way the divinity of God differs from the divinity of Jesus just as sonship describes the way the divinity of Jesus differs from the divinity of God. In fact, the Divine Essence, that is who God is, reduces to the relations of fatherhood and sonship and the relation of the holy spirit reduces to both. After one had described these relations, in other words, there is nothing more to be said about divinity.

In a similar way, the ancient Arabs made so much of familial relationship among their gods, so much in fact, that the man from the Banī Sulaym could ask the Prophet ﷺ: "Tell us your Lord's *nisbah.*" But the Arabs, like all idolaters then as much as today, are absolutely bent on bringing Divinity down to the level of human beings. That is, they are intent on mixing Divine things into the affairs of kinship and pedigree and thereby mixed Divine matters with matters of trade and politics as explained earlier.

Yet, Allāh is ever beyond these earthly affairs. That is why idolatry can never come from exalting the Prophet ﷺ. We cannot exalt him high enough! For how could we mere human beings possibly exalt him higher than Allāh Himself has done? *Shirk,* that is, associating a partner with Allāh, lies in bringing Allāh down to our own low level as if He the Exalted mixed in human affairs like a politicians or business men.

سُبْحَانَ رَبِّكَ رَبِّ الْعِزَّةِ عَمَّا يَصِفُونَ

Subḥān Allāhu ʿamma yaṣifūn

"Glorified be thy Lord, the Lord of Majesty,
transcending what they attribute [to Him]."
(37:180)

Allāh tells the idolaters that those things they gaze upon in the sky are not divine. They are only signs of His Divine Sovereignty. He the Exalted declares:

سَنُرِيهِمْ آيَاتِنَا فِي الْآفَاقِ وَفِي أَنفُسِهِمْ حَتَّى يَتَبَيَّنَ لَهُمْ أَنَّهُ الْحَقُّ

"We will show them Our signs (*ayāt*) in all the
regions of the earth and in their own souls until
they clearly see that He is the real." (41:53)

And He says in addition, look not just in the horizons of the cosmos for My signs,

وَفِي الْأَرْضِ آيَاتٌ لِّلْمُوقِنِينَ وَفِي أَنفُسِكُمْ أَفَلَا تُبْصِرُونَ

"And in the earth are signs for those whose faith is
sure and also in yourselves. Can ye not see?"
(51:20-21)

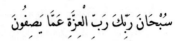

All that is Divine comes down to the relations of partnership the gods have among themselves and with human beings. However, *Sūratu 'l-Ikhlāṣ* explains why Islam show us another path towards the Divine. For the message of Islam is that the Divine Essence cannot be reduced to any set of relations in which Allāh stands to us. But how should we understand this absolute unity of Divine Reality? More specifically, how should we understand it in the context of that Reality's relation to us? This is the subject of the commentary of the individual verses. But before we turn to it, we should note the various names given to *Sūratu 'l-Ikhlāṣ*.

4

The Names of Sūratu 'l-Ikhlāṣ

The commentator on the Qur'ān Fakhru 'd-Dīn ar-Rāzī sums up these names in his *at-Tafsīru 'l-Kabīr* (*The Great Commentary on the Qur'ān*). First, it has been called *Sūratu-t-Tawḥīd* or the *Chapter of Unification*. Now concerning this title, one ought not to forget that "*tawḥīd*" is a causative and intensive noun and never signifies simply an abstract mental state. It is an action, something one does, not simply something one believes and thinks. For it is possible to say that God is one but act as if He is not one by making things other than He one's object of worship: the job, the family, wealth, reputation power or sex. A person can worship all the latter, even give up their life for these things and still say, "I believe there is only on God." *Tawḥīd* as announced by this *sūrah* requires not only that one say that God is one, but to behave accordingly. *Tawḥīd* then is also what Islām is "really" about.

The word "*Islām*" is also a causative and intensive noun. It signifies the act of surrendering, submitting or giving oneself up to another's disposal. A full understanding of *tawḥīd* implies that universal or primordial Islam, submission to God, as the sole Master of destiny and ultimate Reality. Unlike animals, angels, and jinn, the other sentient beings mentioned in the Qur'an, humans are endowed with the capacity to choose. Being endowed with freewill, it is incumbent upon them that their acknowledgement of *tawḥīd* be a matter of choice. The most important sign or token of this acknowledgement is the conscious submission of a person's individual will or ego to the One who is manifestly the Author of all creation. This act of submission is what the Qur'an means by Islam. Only when both the faith and practice of one's Islam are in accord with a full understanding of *tawḥīd* can a person truly be called a Muslim, "one who submits to God." Accordingly, *Sūratu 'l-Ikhlāṣ* is called *Sūratu 'l-Amān,* that is, *Chapter of Safety.*

سورة الامان: قال عليه السلام: " إذا قال العبد لا إله إلا الله دخل حصني ومن دخل حصني أمن من عذابي"

> For the Prophet ﷺ reported Allāh's words when He said, "When the servant utters, *"Lā ilāha illa 'l-Lāh"* (There is no god save the Allāh) he enters under My protection and whoever enters under My protection is safe from My punishment."[12]

For a similar reason, *Sūratu 'l- Ikhlāṣ* is also known as *Sūratu'n-Najāt* or *Chapter of Salvation*; for it saves you from likening anything to Allāh and disbelief in Him in this world and from the fires of Hell in the next.

It is also called *Sūratu 'l-Walāyah.* On this name it is useful to digress for just a moment in order to comment. The root letters making up the word *"Walāyah"* are *W-L-Y,* (*wāw, lām, yā* – و ل ي). They are the same letters that form the word *"walī"* and its plural *"awliyā'."* For lack of a better equivalent in English, I shall translate the latter as "saint," although there is a difference between the nature and function of a *"walī"* in Islam and saints in other religions. The primary meaning of *W-L-Y* in Arabic is proximity or closeness. And these meanings give rise to further meanings. One of these is "to be a friend." The other is "to take charge," "to direct," "to govern." Thus, the *walī* is the friend, he or

[12] Ibid.

she who is close. But *walī*, according to Ibn Manūr in the great Arabic Dictionary *Lisānu 'l-'arab*, is also "he who assists and the *muddabir*, he who manages things." For Allāh gives to those who are His friends some share in the Divine Economy or management of creation according to their rank in His presence. That is why the great expert in traditions (*aḥādīth*) Abū 'Abdi'r-Raḥmān as-Sulamī in *Mināhiju 'l-'arifin* (*The Methods of the Gnostics*) said:

> This is the end (*nihāyah*) of *walāyah*; then there is manifest to the *walī* Divine Favors (*al-karamāt*) in response to his prayers and the reaching to his requests inasmuch as Allāh, The Exalted, does not move [the *walī's* tongue in prayer and questioning except if He causes [the object of the prayer or thing asked for] to come to be.

The phenomenon as-Sulamī describes, by the way, accounts for the word used to described "sainthood" in Islam.

In this connection, sometimes we find "*walāyah*" and sometimes we find "*wilāyah*." Words of latter pattern, the *fi'ālah* pattern in Arabic, signify a function. An example is *khilāfah* or deputyship belonging to humankind spoken of in the Qur'ān. Hence, when the spelling "*wilāyah*" is used, it calls attention to the function the *walī*. For when Allāh declares in *Sūratu 'l-Baqarah* (*Chapter of the Cow*) "Thy Lord said to the angels. 'I am making upon earth a *khalīfah* [i.e., a deputy]" the scholars of Islam say the function of deputyship occurs amongst the *Banī Ādam* (Children of Ādam) in potentiality (*bi 'l-quwwa*) and in actuality (*bi 'l-fi'l*). For Allāh explains that:

وَهُوَ الَّذِي جَعَلَكُمْ خَلَائِفَ الأَرْضِ وَرَفَعَ بَعْضَكُمْ فَوْقَ بَعْضٍ دَرَجَاتٍ

لِّيَبْلُوَكُمْ فِي مَا آتَاكُمْ إِنَّ رَبَّكَ سَرِيعُ الْعِقَابِ وَإِنَّهُ لَغَفُورٌ رَّحِيمٌ

"He it is who made you <u>kh</u>*alā'if* (deputies) of the earth and raised some above others in rank."
(6:165)

Of the ranks of the *actual* deputies are first the prophets at whose head stands the Prophet Muḥammad ﷺ. Being the Perfect Man (*al-Insānu 'l-Kāmil*) he is also the pattern for all the *awliyā'* who come after him.

In any case, the present *sūrah* is called *Sūratu 'l-Walāyah* because whoever reads it becomes amongst Allāh's friends and because whoever knows Allāh in the way described in this *sūrah* has drawn close to Him. For after trial and hardship comes mercy and after Divine Grace comes Divine Favor. The constant reading of this *sūrah* is an essential step on the path to *walāyah* or Sainthood.

Accordingly, it is also known as *Sūratu 'l-Maʿrifah* or *Chapter of Gnosis* inasmuch as the knowledge in the fullest sense or gnosis is not complete without the knowledge contained in this *sūrah*.

روى جابر أن رجلاً صلى فقرأ: قل هو الله أحد فقال النبي عليه الصلاة

والسلام: إن هذا عبد عرف ربه فسميت سورة المعرفة لذلك

The Prophet Muḥammad's ﷺ Companion Jābir relates that a man prayed and read in the course of his prayer "*Qul! Hūwa Allāhu Āḥad* (Say! He is Allāh the Unique). Thereupon the Prophet ﷺ said, "That servant [of God] has full knowledge of his Lord."[13] For that reason, this chapter of the Qur'ān was named "*Suratu 'l-Maʿrifah.*"

[13] *Ibid.*

But one also calls this glorious chapter of the Qur'ān "*Sūratu 'l-Jamāl* or *Chapter of Beauty.*

سورة الجمال قال: عليه الصلاة والسلام: " إن الله جميل يحب الجمال "

فسألوه عن ذلك فقال: أحد صمد لم يلد ولم يولد لأنه إذا لم يكن واحداً

عديم النظير جاز أن ينوب ذلك المثل مناب

> That is because the Prophet ﷺ said, "Surely is Allāh Beauty and He loves what is beautiful." Then those around the Prophet at that moment asked him what he meant. He replied, "*Āḥad ṣamad lām yalid wa-lām yūlad* (Unique Self-Sufficient who does not beget nor is begotten)." [14]

Indeed were He not One without like, then it would possible for something like nature to substitute for Him. And this is clearly impossible.

سورة المقشقشة، يقال: تقشيش المريض مما به، فمن عرف هذا حصل له

البرء من الشرك والنفاق لأن النفاق مرض كما قال : فِى قُلُوبِهِمْ مَّرَضٌ

They call *Sūratu 'l-Ikhlāṣ Sūratu 'l-miqashqashah* or the *Chapter of the Cure,* a cure of a sick person from what afflicts him. One who knows this cure is free from the affliction of associating a partner with Allāh or idolatry. He or she is also cured from hypocrisy, that is, attesting to belief in Allāh and His Prophet ﷺ outwardly whilst believing otherwise within oneself. For hypocrisy is indeed a sickness just as it says in the second *sūrah* of the Qur'ān, *Sūratu 'l-Baqarah* (*Chapter of the Cow*) about the hypocrites that

[14] *Ibid.*

surrounded the Prophet like ʿAbd Allāh ibn Ubayy, "They have in their hearts a sickness (*fī qulūbihim maraḍ*)." (2:12)

المعوذة، روى أنه عليه السلام دخل على عثمان بن مظعون فعوذه بها

وباللتين بعدها، ثم قال: " نعوذ بهن فما تعوذت بخير منها

In addition, *Sūratu 'l-Ikhlāṣ* is named *Sūratu 'l-Muʿawwidhah*, the *Chapter of Refuge*. It is narrated that the Prophet ﷺ entered upon ʿUthmān ibn Maẓʿūn ؓ whilst he was taking refuge in its protection along with the *sūrahs* that follow it. Thereupon, the Prophet ﷺ gave the order, "Take refuge in their protection! For that in which you have taken refuge is a goodness due to them."[15] He meant the three last chapters of the Qur'ān of which *Sūratu 'l-Ikhlāṣ* is the first. The other two are *Sūratu'-Falaq* (*Chapter of the Daybreak*) then *Sūratu'n-Nās*(*Chapter of Humankind*).

سورة الصمد لأنها مختصة بذكره تعالى

It is called *Sūratu'ṣ-ṣamad* because it mentions that name of Allāh, *aṣ-ṣamad*.

سورة الصمد لأنها مختصة بذكره تعالى

But our chapter was also given the name *Sūratu 'l-Asās* or the *Chapter of the Foundation*. For the Prophet ﷺ said reporting a Divine Saying: "I have founded the seven heavens and seven earths upon '*Qul! Hūwa Allāhu Āḥad*' [i.e., upon 'Say! He is Allāh the Unique']." [16] And according to Imām Rāzī, the evidence for this is the statement that three causes of the destruction of the

[15] Ibid.
[16] Ibid.

heavens and the earth mentioned in the Qur'ān where Allāh declares in *Sūrah Maryam* (*Chapter of Mary*) at verses:

وَقَالُوا اتَّخَذَ الرَّحْمَنُ وَلَدًا لَقَدْ جِئْتُمْ شَيْئًا إِدًّا تَكَادُ السَّمَاوَاتُ يَتَفَطَّرْنَ مِنْهُ وَتَنشَقُّ الْأَرْضُ وَتَخِرُّ الْجِبَالُ هَدًّا أَن دَعَوْا لِلرَّحْمَنِ وَلَدًا

> And they say, The All-Merciful One (sc. God) has taken unto Himself a son. Assuredly, you utter a disastrous thing, whereby almost the heaves are torn, and the earth is split asunder and the mountains fall into ruins, that you ascribe unto the All-Merciful One a son. (19: 88-91)

For it is necessary that *tawḥīd* be the building blocks (*'imārah*) of the heavens, the earth and the mountains. To understand this point we only have to imagine a building constructed by many different builders each following a different plan. How can we expect such a building to stand? Imām Rāzī reports that some say the cause mentioned is the meaning of Allāh's statement in *Sūratu 'l-Anbiyā'* (*Chapter of the Prophets*):

لَوْ كَانَ فِيهِمَا آلِهَةٌ إِلَّا اللَّهُ لَفَسَدَتَا فَسُبْحَانَ اللَّهِ رَبِّ الْعَرْشِ عَمَّا يَصِفُونَ

> If there were gods therein beside Allāh, then truly both [the heavens and the earth] had been disordered. Glory be to Allāh, the Lord of the Throne, from all that they ascribe to Him. (21:22)

سورة المانعة روى ابن عباس أنه تعالى قال :لنبيه حين عرج به أعطيتك

سورة الإخلاص وهي من ذخائر كنوز عرشي، وهي المانعة تمنع عذاب

القبر ولفحات النيران

In addition, *Sūratu 'l-Ikhlāṣ* is called *Sūratu 'l-Māni'ah* or the *Chapter of Prevention*. It is narrated on the authority of Ibn 'Abbās that Allāh said to the Prophet ﷺ when He caused him on that Night *Isrā'* (night journey) and *Mi'rāj* (ascension) to ascend unto His Divine Presence, "I have granted unto you *Sūratu 'l- Ikhlāṣ* and it is from the armaments belonging to the treasures of My Throne and it is a preventative that wards off the punishment of the grave and the scorching fires of Hell."[17]

Sūratu 'l- Ikhlāṣ having been bestowed upon the Prophet ﷺ in so sublime a setting, it is not surprising that it is known also by the title *Sūratu 'l-Ḥaḍr*, the *Chapter of Presence* because the angels make themselves present to listen to it whenever it is read. In contrast to that, *Sūratu 'l- Ikhlāṣ* is at the same time named *"al-munaffirah"* — *"the repellant"* because when it is read, Satan runs away. The Prophet ﷺ, therefore, called *Sūratu 'l-Ikhlāṣ* an instrument of absolution.

روي أنه عليه السلام رأى رجل يقرأ هذه السورة، فقال: أما هذا فقد

بريء من الشرك، وقال عليه السلام: من قرأ سورة قل هو الله أحد مائة

مرة في صلاة أو في غيرها كتبت له براءة من النار

[17] Ibid.

> It is narrated that he ﷺ saw a man reading this chapter of the Qur'ān and he said, "This man is innocent of idolatry by associating a partner to Allāh. He ﷺ said in addition that, "Whoever reads '*Qul! Hūwa Allāhu Āḥad*' ('Say! He is Allāh the Unique') a hundred times during the course of his prayer or at some other time it has been written for him absolution from the punishment of Hellfire." [18]

They name it also *Sūratu 'l-Mudhdhakirah*, "The Reminding Chapter" because it causes the servant or handmaid pure their practice of *tawḥīd* to call Allāh into remembrance with their tongues. For reading of *Sūratu 'l-Ikhlāṣ* is like placing a rubberband upon the arm or tying a string around your finger to remind you of what you have need to remember but have tendency to neglect. Yet, there is no neglect more serious that forgetfulness of Allāh, since in forgetting Him we forget ourselves, that is, who we are as creatures. It is difficult to imagine an identity crisis greater than this, not to know who you are.

After all, identities we assume, son, daughter, father, mother, citizen, subject, teacher, doctor, blacksmith, CEO, etc. All these fade and pass away. Our identities as creatures, servants and handmaids to Allāh never fade. That is why, Allāh says in *Sūratu 'l-Ḥashr:*

وَلَا تَكُونُوا كَالَّذِينَ نَسُوا اللَّهَ فَأَنسَاهُمْ أَنفُسَهُمْ أُولَٰئِكَ هُمُ الْفَاسِقُونَ

"Be not like those who forgot Allāh, then He caused them to forget themselves; such are the evil-doers. " (59:19)

[18] Ibid.

It is impossible for the human being to know himself and not to know Allāh. Our identities as humans is thus bound up with Allāh.

مَنْ عَرَفَ نَفْسَهُ فَقَدْ عَرَفَ رَبَّهُ

> Accordingly, the Prophet ﷺ said, "Whoever know himself, know his Lord."[19]

In what way this is so will unfold as the commentary proceeds.

But for now we note another name for *Sūratu 'l-Ikhlāṣ*. It is *Sūratu'n-Nūr*. Allāh says in the chapter that has that title as its primary designation,

اللَّهُ نُورُ السَّمَاوَاتِ وَالْأَرْضِ

"Allāh is the Light of the heavens and the Earth." (24:35)

He, the Exalted, is the one who illumines the heaven and earth. *Sūratu 'l-Ikhlāṣ* illumines your heart.

وقال عليه السلام: " إن لكل شيء نور ونور القرآن قل هو الله أحد

The Prophet ﷺ said, "Everything has a light and the light of the Qur'ān is '*Qul! Hūwa Allāhu Āḥad*' ('Say! He is Allāh the

[19] There is dispute as regards to this particular tradition. As-Suyuti quoted Imam an-Nawawi in his *Jami*, said it is not established. The famous Sufis are known for using this tradition, like Ibn 'Arabi who was defended by ash-Shaykh Hijazi, the commentator or the *Jami*, counted Ibn 'Arabi among the huffaz who said about traditions that weren't transmitted by the way of isnad:

وإن لم يصح من طريق الرواية فقد صح عندنا م طريق الكشف

Surely it isn't sound by the way of riwayah, for us it is sound from the way of unveiling

Unique')."[20] He compares it to the light of the human individual in the smallest of his or her members, that is, the pupil of the eye. Thus, this *sūra* is to the Qur'ān what the pupil of the eye is to man (*fa-ṣārati-s-sūratu li'-l-Qurāni ka 'l-ḥadaqti li 'l-insāni*). Imām ar-Rāzī thus plays upon the word for man in Arabic "*insān*" which can also mean "pupil of the eye" (*insānu 'l-'ayn*).

A Deeper Look

To see the importance of the analogy drawn between this *sūra* and light we only have to ask ourselves: How can there be a creation that is unwitnessed (*hal kāna 'l-khalq bi-dūna 'l-mushāhadati*)? And how can there be a witnessing without light? This does not mean that a person can only affirm his or her own perceived existence as the only reality. This is not what is meant when we say creation requires a witnessing.

The secret here lies enfolded in the Arabic language. Arabic unlike English allows no radical separation between existing for "me" and existing for "everybody else." The English sentences "Such-and-such exists" or "x is there" are always neutral. They do not imply that there must be someone there to witness that a thing exists. The term for being or existence in Arabic "*wujūd,*" however, is different. Derived from the root *W-J-D*, it means, "to find," "the act of finding" as well as "being found." But in order for something to be found, there must be someone there to find it. So in the Arabic word "*wujūd*" there is also always an underlying sense of presence of conscious life, the sense of something perceived or witnessed.

Accordingly, among the *Ahlu 't-Tawḥīd*, the masters of unification, the term "*wujūd*" is used with two others words, derived from the same root, "*tawājud*" and "*wajd.*" In the context of their science,

[20] Rāzī in his *Mafātīḥ*.

the first signifies the seeking of *wajd* or the powerful and overwhelming feeling that one has found oneself in the Divine Presence. The second signifies the actual sense of finding oneself in the Divine Presence. It pervades the heart (*qalb*), psyche (*nafs*) and the bodily framework (*jawāriḥ*). Recall, what we heard Imām al-Ghazālī say earlier: "Tasting is finding (*wajdān*)."

Imām al-Qushayrī's discusses in his famous *Risālah* of the subtle interrelation of these three terms:

ما الوجود: فهو بعد الارتقاء عن الوجد. ولا يكون وجود الحق، إلا بعد خمور البشرية، لأنه لا يكون للبشرية بقاء عند ظهور سلطان الحقيق وهذا معنى قول أبي الحسين النوري: أنا منذ عشرين سنة بين الوجد والفقد: أي: إذا وجدت ربيَّ فقدت قلبي، وإذا وجدت قلبي فقدت ربي.

وهذا معنى قول الجنيد: علم التوحيد: مباين لوجوده، ووجوده مباين لعلمه.

وفي هذا المعنى أنشدوا:

وجودي أن أغيب عن الوجود   بما يبدو عليَّ من الشهود

فالتواجد: بداية. والوجود: نهاية والوجد واسطة بين البداية والنهاية.

سمعت الأستاذ أبا علي الدقاق يقول: التواجد يوجب استغراق العبد.

والوجود يوجب استهلاك العبد . فهو كمن شهد البحر، ثم ركب البحر، ثم غرق في البحر وترتيب هذا الأمر: قصود، ثم ورود، ثم شهود، ثم جمود، ثم خمود . وبمقدار الوجود يحصل الخمود، وصاحب الوجود له: صحو، ومحو.

As for *wujūd*, it comes after ascent from *wajd*. For the *wujūd al-Ḥaqq* [i.e., the existence of Allāh, the Real] only arrives after the extinction of one's human characteristics (*ba'da khumūd al-basharīyya*). For it is impossible for one to continue to abide (*baqā'*) after the appearance of the *Sulṭānu 'l-Ḥaqīqah* (the power of Reality.) That is what Abū'l- Hasan an-Nūrī meant when he said: "For the twenty past years I am betwixt finding (*wajd*) and losing (*faqd*). That is, if I find my heart, I lose my Lord." This is also the meaning of al-Junayd's statement to the effect that, "Knowledge of God's *tawḥīd* causes his existence (*wujūd*) to vanish and His Existence (*wujūd*) causes knowledge of Him to vanish." On this point a poet recites "My *wujūd* is that I be absent from *wujūd* insofar as there is appearance in me of *shuhūd*." Thus, *tawājud* is the beginning, *wujūd* is the end, while *wajd* is the midpoint between the point of departure and the end. I heard my master Abū 'Alī ad-Daqqāq say: "*Tawḥīd* requires the servant's total application, *wajd* his absorption, *wujūd* his destruction (*istihlāk*). It is like a person who beholds the sea, then travels on it, then, is drowned in it. And the order [of

> occurrence] is thus: [the servant's] setting out to see (*quṣūd*), then an appearance (*wurūd*), then witnessing (*shuhūd*), then *wujūd*, then extinction (*khumūd*). And one possesses *wujūd* according to the intensity of extinction from one's human characteristics.

The apparent paradox in the hemistich, "My *wujūd* (existence) is that I be absent from *wujūd* (existence)" plays upon the sense contained in the root *W-J-D*—"to be found there." In order for something to be found, it must be *there* to be found. But Imām al-Qushayrī's point is that after the appearance of the *Sulṭānu 'l-Ḥaqīqah*, there is no there *there*. Being there in this case does not exist.

So, when the servant forms an intention to set out to see (*quṣūd*), there is no seeing without appearing (*wurūd*) and no *wujūd* without *shuhūd*. That is why the *Āhlu 't-Tawḥīd* gloss the Prophet's ﷺ definition of *iḥsān* in the way they do. Defining *Iḥsān* or doing good, when questioned by Jibrīl ﷺ concerning the five pillars of Islam, he ﷺ said. "It is to worship Allāh as though you see Him; for if you are not seeing Him, He sees you." The *Āhlu 't-Tawḥīd* say, if you want a short-cut to the real meaning of this ḥadīth, then stop after the words "for if you are not," (*fa in lām takun*) then "you see Him" (*tarāh*).

What this means is that when your existence is negated, (*lām takun*), in the state of *fanā*, then Allāh grants the beatific vision of the Divine Presence.

For in the final analysis the important thing is not that you bear witness to Allāh's existence in the act of *shahādah* and say "*Lā ilāha illa 'l-Lāh*" (There is no god save Allāh). That is only a beginning. What is important is that Allāh sees you. But He sees you when you are not. And that means, if you do not exist in your human characteristics (*bas̲h̲arīyya*), Allāh sees you. We achieve our real identity, when we know who we are in the sight of Allāh, not in the sight of humankind (*al-bas̲h̲arīyya*).

At the beginning we only act as if we exist, just as we may pretend to be in love. As Imām al-Qus̲h̲ayrī's master Abū ʿAlī ad-Daqqāq said, it is a period of total application in *d̲h̲ikr* or frequent mentioning of Allāh, through spiritual exercises by reciting offices (*awrād*), standing to pray at night (*qiyāmu 'l-layl*), reading the Qur'ān, etc. Then, there is *wajd*. It is like the standing outside oneself in a state of ecstasy. One is absorbed not in oneself but with Allāh. Finally, there is *wujūd* or destruction or extinction of the ego. Still, this knowledge of the Lord will bestow a level of consciousness where the knower will no longer be able to distinguish who knows from what is known.

According to Imām al-G̲h̲azālī: "Abū Bakr aṣ-Ṣiddīq ﷺ alluded to this when he said: "Powerlessness to attain knowledge is a perception." Literally it means, "The incapacity to catch hold of perception is [itself] a perception." Thus, Abū Bakr indicates that the knowledge one attains after self-knowledge may be knowledge of one's incapacity to attain knowledge of Allāh. This too is a level of knowledge and one that is very profound. For knowledge of Allāh absorbs the knower totally and yet it is as if he or she has perceived scarcely anything at all, so infinite is that ocean. This may persist until the servant has lost track of his or her own existence. Then, at the point there is no knowledge or perceiving who is the knower or perceiver and who the known or the perceived. And this is what the Prophet ﷺ meant when he said, "I reckon no praise of You like Your praise of Yourself."[21]

[21]

Now according to the *Ahlu 't-Tawḥīd,* among them Imāms ash-Shiblī and Abū-Ḥāmid al-Ghazālī, the ḥadīth,

خَلَقَ اللهُ عَزَّ وَجَل آدَمَ على صُورَتِه

"Allāh created Adam according to His own form (*ʿalā ṣūratihi*)"[22]

means man was created according to the Names and Attributes. It does not mean he was created according to Allāh's Essence. The *muwaḥḥidūn*— those who put into realization of Allāh's Oneness in their lives — distinguish between *Hāhūt, Lahūt* and *Nasūt. Hāhūt* is the transcendent, unattainable Essence and corresponds to *Hūwa Allāhu Āḥad* as we will see and *Lāhūt* is part of that Divine Realm.

But *Nasūt* is the garment (*kiswah*) of the eternal witness (*shāhidu 'l-qidam*) in which the human form was dressed when pledging the Covenant on the Day of Promises. Thus, Allāh refers to the Prophet ﷺ when he declares:

يَا أَيُّهَا النَّبِيُّ إِنَّا أَرْسَلْنَاكَ شَاهِدًا وَمُبَشِّرًا وَنَذِيرًا

"O Prophet! Truly, We have sent you as a witness (*shāhid).*" (33:45)

It means He has dressed His creature with the garment (*kiswah*) of His Divine Names and Attributes.

Right after the passage quoted above Imām al-Qushayrī strikes the same theme and continues with the end of the famous ḥadīth qudsī where Allāh says that when He loves His servant, "I am his hearing with which he hears, the seeing with which he sees..." Only Allāh can say this because according to the Prophet ﷺ,

[22] Al-Bukhārī from Abū Hurayrah ؓ.

"Allāh created Adam according to His own form (*'alā ṣūratihi*)."[23] And the servant who has entered the state (*ḥāl*) of "*Ta<u>kh</u>allaqū*," I mean, whoever has fulfilled the Prophetic command:

تخلقوا بأخلاق الله

> "*Takhallaqū bi-akhlāqi 'l-Lah*" -"Put on the character traits of Allāh!"[24]

saves his soul out of the veil of the sea of creation. For he or she is "like a person who beholds the sea, then travels on it, then, is drowned in it."

At that moment, such a one will behold the beauty (*Jamāl*) of Allāh in the nowhere that bears no traces (*rusūm*). Then the servant will become the guest of the *tajallī* of the verse in the Qur'ān:

وَلَكِنِ انظُرْ إِلَى

"*Lakini 'nẓur ilā 'l-jabal*"

قَالَ لَن تَرَانِي وَلَكِنِ انظُرْ إِلَى الْجَبَلِ

Do thou but look to the mountain (7:143)

answering the request of the Prophet Mūsā ﷺ to behold his Lord. The verse reads:

وَلَمَّا جَاء مُوسَى لِمِيقَاتِنَا وَكَلَّمَهُ رَبُّهُ قَالَ رَبِّ أَرِنِي أَنظُرْ إِلَيْكَ قَالَ لَن تَرَانِي وَلَكِنِ انظُرْ إِلَى الْجَبَلِ فَإِنِ اسْتَقَرَّ مَكَانَهُ فَسَوْفَ تَرَانِي فَلَمَّا تَجَلَّى رَبُّهُ لِلْجَبَلِ جَعَلَهُ دَكًّا وَخَرَّ موسَى صَعِقًا

"And when Mūsā came (*jā'a*) to Our appointed tryst and his Lord had spoken unto him, he said,

23

24 Al-Ghazzālī reported this in his *Iḥyā'* and ash-Sha'rānī in his *Ṭabaqāt*.

My Lord Show me [Thyself] that I may behold
Thee." However, "'When his Lord disclosed
Himself (*tajalla*) to the mountain, He rendered it
dust and Mūsā ﷺ fell down senseless (7:143)."

Now the verse says, "Mūsā came" (*jā'a*). But of Muḥammad the Qur'ān says that Allāh "carried His servant by night (*asrā bi ʿabdihi*)." (17:1) "Coming" is not the same as "being carried." In this way' the Qur'ān draws our attention to the fact that Prophet Muḥammad ﷺ, was the only Prophet to ascend into the Divine Presence. The Qur'ān tells us that upon the Divine Self-manifestation or *tajallī* to the mountain, "Mūsā fell down senseless (7:143)." Yet, when the Prophet Muḥammad ﷺ went on the *isrā'* and *miʿrāj*, no such physical effect is reported. Why was this? It was because of our liegelord Muḥammad's self-annihilation in Divine Love. Or as Abu ʿAlī ad-Daqqāq says above, "his *wujūd* [became] his destruction (*istihlāk*)" for the servant cannot endure the sun of the Allāh's Divine Majesty (*Jalāl*).

So as a guest of the Divine Self-disclosure or *tajallī* contained in this *āyah* Allāh shows His servant this world clad in the form of Muḥammad ﷺ. That is, Allāh shows the servant His creation in the Muhammadan Light (*nūr Muḥammadī*). For there is no witnessing (*shuhūd*) without light. As said in the quotation from Imām al-Qushayrī, "*shuhūd* precedes *wujūd* in the servant's ascent to his Lord. In consequence, after declaring,

يَا أَيُّهَا النَّبِيُّ إِنَّا أَرْسَلْنَاكَ شَاهِدًا وَمُبَشِّرًا وَنَذِيرًا وَدَاعِيًا إِلَى اللهِ بِإِذْنِهِ
وَسِرَاجًا مُّنِيرًا

"O Prophet! Truly We have sent you as a Witness
(*shāhid*)" Allāh continues the verse and adds, "and

as a Lamp spreading Light (*sirājan munīra*)." (33:45-46)

And in another place, He says:

قَدْ جَاءَكُم مِّنَ اللّهِ نُورٌ وَكِتَابٌ مُّبِينٌ

"From Allāh has come to you a Light and a Book manifest." (5:15)

According to Imām Ibn Jarīr aṭ-Ṭabarī in his *Tafsīr Jāmiʿ al-Bayān* says that in the latter verse:

يعني بالنور محمد صلى الله عليه وسلم، الذي أنار الله به الحق

"He means by the Light: Muḥammad ﷺ by means of whom Allāh has illuminated the truth."

Similarly, Shaykh Ismāʿīl al-Ḥaqqī al-Bursawī comments:

وقيل المراد بالاول هو الرسول صلى الله عليه وسلم وبالثانى القرآن

There has come to you a Light from Allāh and a Book that makes all things manifest"- It is said that the meaning of the former is the Messenger ﷺ and the latter is the Qur'ān... The Messenger ﷺ is called a Light because the first thing which Allāh brought forth from the darkness of oblivion with the light of His power was the light of Muḥammad as he ﷺ said, "The first thing Allāh created is my light."'

He alludes, of course, to the famous ḥadīth handed down from Jābir ibn ʿAbd Allāh who inquired of the Prophet, saying:

رواه عبد الرزاق بسنده عن جابر بن عبد الله بلفظ قال قلت: يا رسول

الله، بأبي أنت وأمي، أخبرني عن أول شيء خلقه الله قبل الأشياء.

قال: يا جابر، إن الله تعالى خلق قبل الأشياء نور نبيك من نوره، فجعل

ذلك النور يدور بالقُدرة حيث شاء الله، ولم يكن في ذلك الوقت لوح ولا

قلم ولا جنة ولا نار ولا ملك ولا سماء ولا أرض ولا شمس ولا قمر ولا

جِنّيٌ ولا إنسي، فلما أراد الله أن يخلق الخلق قسم ذلك النور أربعة

أجزاء: فخلق من الجزء الأول القلم، ومن الثاني اللوح، ومن الثالث

العرش...

"O Messenger of Allāh! I have given up my father and mother for you! But please tell me about the first thing Allāh created before all things." The Prophet ﷺ replied: "O Jabir! The first thing Allāh created was the light of your Prophet from His light. That light abided, turning in the midst of His Power for as long as He wished. At that time, there was no Tablet nor Pen, nor Paradise nor Hell-Fire. There was neither an angel nor a heaven nor an earth. When Allāh then, wished to create creation, he divided that Light into four parts. From the first He created the Pen, from the second the Tablet, from the third the Throne, [and from the fourth everything else]."[25]

Also, the famous authority on the Qur'an the Prophet's Companion Ibn 'Abbās ◈ reports:

---

[25] 'Abdur-Razzaq in his *Musannaf* from Jābir.

> Verily the spirit of the Prophet ﷺ was a light in front of Allāh two thousands years before he created Adam. That light glorified Him and the angels joined in its glorification. When Allāh created Adam, he cast that light into his loins.[26]

The great Qur'an commentator Sahl at-Tustarī echoes these traditions in his *tafsīr*:

> God created the light of Muḥammad out of his own light... That light dwelt before God for a hundred thousand years. He directed His gaze towards it seventy times each day and each night, adding a new light with each glance. After it, He created all creatures.

But as ad-Daylamī tells us:

> When Allāh looks at a thing, He makes in it an image from Him and that image will remain through all eternity and in that image will remain ...all His Attributes.

Each time that Allāh looked upon the Prophet ﷺ He dressed him with more of the Names and Attributes by which He expressed His Essence. He clothed him with names like ar-Raḥmān, ar-Raḥīm, al-Ghafūr, ar-Ra'ūf, and many more. For He also clothed him with different Names and Attributes, with which He dressed no one else. That is why the Prophet ﷺ has countless names given to him by Allāh.

Clad with *akhlāqu 'l-Ḥaqq*, the character traits of Allāh, Allāh commanded him:

26

وَقُلْ جَاءَ الْحَقُّ وَزَهَقَ الْبَاطِلُ إِنَّ الْبَاطِلَ كَانَ زَهُوقًا

Qul! jā'a al-ḥaq wa-zahiqa bāṭil.
"Say [O Muḥammad!] Truth has come and
falsehood hath vanished." (17:81)

To whom does "al-Ḥaqq" refer in this verse? Commentators say Muḥammad is al-Ḥaqq. At that moment, then, when his spirituality and heavenly power descended on the Prophet ﷺ, Reality appeared, certainty was seen and everything *bāṭil,* false, evanesced into nothingness. Allāh dressed him with the Divine Attribute al-Ḥaqq, clothing him simultaneously with the light of the holy Qur'ān.

وأخرج ابن أبي شيبة وعبد بن حميد ومسلم وابن المنذر والحاكم وابن مردويه عن سعد بن هشام قال: أتيت عائشة فقلت يا أم المؤمنين: أخبرني بخلق رسول الله صلى الله عليه وسلم، فقالت: كان خلقه القرآن، أما تقرأ القرآن ﴿وإنك لعلى خلق عظيم﴾

For this reason, when the Mother of Believers, Sayyidatunā 'Ā'isha ؓ, the Prophet's wife was asked, "What were the character traits of the Messenger of Allāh?" his wife replied, "Have you read the Qur'ān?" His character was the Qur'an (*kāna khuluqahu 'l-Qur'ān*)."[27]

[27] Muslim, al-Ḥākim, Ibn Abī Shaybah, 'Abd ibn Ḥumayd, al-Mardaway from S'ad ibn Hāshim ؓ.

> Or in another report, "His character traits were perfect congruent with the Qur'ān (*khuluquhu li 'l-qur'āni muwaffaq*)."[28]

The Prophet was the Qur'ān alive and walking about. It means that the character of the Messenger of Allāh is the Qur'ān and the assumption of the Divine Names as his names. Allāh said of the Prophet ﷺ:

وَإِنَّكَ لَعَلَى خُلُقٍ عَظِيمٍ

"Surely, thou art of tremendous character (*khuluqin aẓīm*)" (68:4)

just as He gave His book the description:

وَالْقُرْآنَ الْعَظِيمَ

"the tremendous Qur'ān." (15:87)

So the character of Muḥammad ﷺ is the Qur'ān.

Now when Allāh took the Prophet ﷺ to that station, he made him ever-living in his everlastingness. And when Allāh raised him up He annihilated Him in His Divines Names (*fa-qad fani'a fī'l-Lāhi fa-qadhafanī fī 'l-Lāh*). At the same time, however, the Divine Names seek disclosure in the cosmos just as a lamp seeks to illumine dark room. Is it not in the nature of *an-Nūr* as Light to shine forth? Thus, how can *al-Ḥaqq* remain hidden?

Truth cannot help but manifest itself. Otherwise, it is not truth. And what, after all, is *nūr*? We see by means of it. But how can we describe it? If you turn off all the lights, you see nothing. It becomes dark. We say light of the sun (*nūru' sh-Shams*). If the sun does not appear the day doesn't come and it is night. You see

28

nothing except, perhaps, the moonlight (*nūru 'l-qamar*). But if the moon does not appear, then we are plunged into total darkness.

In that very moment, the Prophet ﷺ understood his limits. He understood, in one fell swoop, the full meaning of "*lā sharīka 'l-Lāh*," the precise sense in which Allāh has no partner. It was this understanding that swept him away and caused his utter extinction in Allāh. When the Prophet ﷺ saw that reality and understood it, he knew there was no more any existence for him and cried out, "Yā Rabbī! I am your servant! *Yā Rabbī!* I am nothing."

When someone dies, we soften the effect by saying he or she he expired or passed away. But it means the same thing: That person no longer lives. He has no existence. He is not real anymore. Time loses existence every second that it moves forward. In reality, however, time has no existence. With Allāh there is neither time nor place. And even with us time is less and less real to us. Therefore it has no reality. Today we are here. Tomorrow we are not here. It means our existence is gone, finished. Who then is real? Who is lasting forever? The one that exists forever: Allāh.

When the Prophet ﷺ saw all that he understood it, he knew there is no existence for him. Upon that realization, he reached annihilation. That is why when he went on *isrā'* and *miʿrāj*, there was no physical effect on him. Today they say don't go high on the mountain or you will develop high blood pressure. So how did the Prophet ﷺ go on that journey through space? It was because he became annihilated in Divine Love. When Allāh took him to that station, he made him ever lasting in His ever lastingness.

Now the "*wujūdu 'l-Ḥaqīqah*" Imām al-Qushayrī has told us, "only arrives after the extinction of *basharīyya* (human characteristics)," since at this station, no one exists except Allāh. In this way, the physical features of *nasūt* with the Prophet ﷺ declined and the power of *lāhūt* grew ever stronger and came finally to dominate him utterly. For when that Divine source of power was laid open to him, he was physically transfigured. That is, his physicality declined and his heavenly power increased dominating his physical aspect. At that time he was able to take hold of that heavenly power.

How this is so becomes clearer when we reflect on the last of the names of *Sūratu 'l-Ikhlāṣ* to be considered. That name emerged from an occasion in which *Sūratu 'l-Ikhlāṣ* was revealed, as reported in a tradition handed down on the authority of ʿAbd Allāh ibn Masʿūd. I alluded to this earlier. A man from a tribe called the Banī Sulaym, asked of the Prophet ﷺ, "Give us your Lord's lineage (*nisbah*)." There descended in answer, "Say: He is Allāh, the Unique..." The sūrah revealed thus became known as *Sūratu'n-Nisbah.*

Of course, the Arabs of those days paid a great deal of attention to matters of kinship and pedigree. The man from the Banī Sulaym was asking about Allāh's genealogy in the network of socio-economic relationships spoken of earlier. He wanted to know where Allāh stood in the family of Arabian gods. According to Imām Abū Ḥāmid al-Ghazālī, "The meaning is that Allāh's relationship is too holy, too transcendent for any idea of lineage [that the man had in mind]." So when the Prophet replied: "O Brother of the Banī Sulaym, making Allāh's *nisbah* your business is better." He ﷺ meant the relationship Allāh has described Himself as having with His creatures through His Beautiful Names. So, the Prophet ﷺ in answering Him, is saying pre-occupy yourself with the relation that Allāh stands to him instead concerning himself with Divine Genealogy. For Allāh is Unique; He is not born nor begotten.

To the Prophet ﷺ the term *"nisbah"* meant the relation of Allāh to His creation as revealed by His Attributes. Each attribute shows a way in which Allāh relates to us. He is All Merciful (*ar-Raḥmān*) to us; He is our Creator (*al-Khāliq*), and so on. All the Divine Names describe the relation of Allāh to us. For each, the Divine Name implies a relationship in which Allāh stands to His creation.
For example, the name *"an-Nur"* the Light, implies a relation to something illuminated or *al-munawwar,* something in need of illumination. Thus, *an-Nūr* only exists insofar as creation is in an interdependent relation with perception. Shaykhu 'l-Ishrāq or the Master of Illumination, Shihābu 'd-Dīn as-Suhrawardī al-Maqtūl accordingly takes the Divine Name, *an-Nūr* as describing an illuminative relation (*iḍāfatu 'l-ishrāqīyya*). Such a relation depicts a variation of intensity in light becoming fainter as the distance from Divine Light increases, but never separating from that source or becoming detached from it.
In discussing the causes behind the revelation of *Sūratu 'l-Ikhlāṣ* we read about how the people of the Jews came to the Prophet ﷺ saying, "O Muḥammad! This Allāh hath fashioned creation. But who created Allāh?" *"Qul: Hūwa Allāh Āḥad..."* was revealed. Then they said: "What power, what strength hath He in his forearm? and Jibrīl brought the verse (6:91),

وَمَا قَدَرُوا اللّهَ حَقَّ قَدْرِه

"They measured not the power of Allāh its true measure (*mā qadara 'l-Lāha haqqa qadrihi*)," i.e., "They have not known Allāh according to a true knowledge of Him (*mā arafu 'l- Lāha ḥaqqa ma'rifatihi*)."

But what constitutes a true knowledge of Allāh? The idolaters, of course, had made gods of the created powers of nature, the rising sun, the moon, the stars and so on. As the Qur'ān tells us, this they did on the basis of knowledge passed down from their forefathers as they told the Prophet Ibrāhīm when he asked them, "'What are these images unto which ye pay devotion?" They said, "We found our fathers worshippers of them."[29] Similarly, recall also the words of the delegation of idolaters of the Quraysh to Muḥammad ﷺ, "You have broken ranks with our community, provoked our divinities and abandoned the religion of your forefathers." For idolatry is the same in every age. It is based on knowledge passed down on the tongues of men, not heart-knowledge.

Human knowledge cannot grasp the Divine Essence. Hence, whoever searches for a means to know his or her Lord, must, as said earlier, take a *wasīlah*. But the *wasīlah* for us takes the form of a mirror. This mirror will reflect the *tajalliyāt*, that is, the Divine Disclosures of the Names and Attributes upon the soul of the Prophet ﷺ.

[29] 21:53

5

Commentary

قُلْ هُوَ اللَّهُ أَحَدٌ

That is, "Say: He is Allāh, the Unique." "*Qul*" or "say," is the first word of *Sūratu 'l-Ikhlāṣ* after the beginning *bismi 'l-Lāhi 'r-Raḥmāni 'r-Raḥīm* (In the name of Allāh, the All-Merciful, the Compassionate). It is a command (*amr*), an order given to inform others of what follows. In this case, it also assigns Muḥammad ﷺ the status of Messenger (*rasūl*) and Prophet (*nabī*).

The peculiarity of that status requires that the message reach a larger audience than those who were immediately with the Prophet ﷺ at the moment of revelation. Understanding of his special role is what caused him to predict even in his own time, "there will remain no house in a settled nor tent in a desert that Islam will not enter."[30] We see this happening today. The name of Allāh and the name of Muḥammad ﷺ are upon people's lips. People everywhere are talking about the Qur'ān. They read it, even though they are not Muslim. Where did the Prophet ﷺ receive this foreknowledge that Islam was going to enter every dwelling? Neither Mūsa ؑ nor 'Īsa ؑ can boast this order of predictive power for their messages.

Directly following the command "*Qul!*" is "*Hūwa*" (He)." In Arabic "*hūwa*" is a masculine third-person-singular pronoun. From the commentators we learn the grammatical role of "*hūwa*" in this *sūrah*. They say, "*hūwa*" in this context functions as a "pronoun of the fact (*ḍamīru 'sh-sha'n*) or "pronoun of the story

[30] Al-Ḥākim's *Mustadrak*.

(*ḍamīru 'l-qissah*). For it refers to the entire subsequent clause and in this way anticipates it, namely the clause, "*Allāhu Āḥad*." Thus, "*hūwa*" is the subject and its predicate is the entire clause (*jumlah*) following it. It is possible that "*hūwa*" refers back to something understood from the conversation prior to it.

Recall, the idolaters, the Jews and the Christians had demanded: "Make clear to us the kind (*jins*) of object you worship (*ma'būdaka*)." and "O Messenger of Allāh! Describe to us your Lord, what He is (*ṣif lanā rabbaka mā hūwa*)" and "Relate (*unsub*) concerning your Lord to us!" So, "*hūwa*" may refer back to their request. There is, however, no need for backward reference. The clause identifies the fact expressed by the pronoun, namely, "*Allāhu Āḥad*."

But in general "*hūwa*" always refers to something unidentified. That is, as a third person pronoun it does not directly identify its referent, unlike the person singular pronoun "*anā*." To enter a room and say "I am not here" is to immediately utter a paradox. The same is not true if one says, "He is not here" since "he" does not wear its identity on its sleeve so to speak, at least, not in the same way "I" does. Hence, the third person singular pronoun can signify an absence, or something one may not wish to describe or cannot describe. In this *sūrah,* however, its use indicates that one does not wish to identify its referent of "*hūwa*." There is a reason for this. "*Hūwa*" as used here signifies that one cannot know the Divine Identity or *Dhāt*, or who God is in His real nature or essence. Or, as the scholars or '*ulamā*' say, one cannot specify its *huwīyya* or is-ness that is, the identity or selfhood of the referent.

Now we hear psychologists say that so-and-so, usually an adolescent is undergoing an identity crisis. That is, the person does not know who he or she is. Their selfhood is lost to them. Another word the Arabs use for self is *dhāt*. They pronounce it exactly the way we pronounce the word "that." One can also translate dhāt as essence. But dhāt denotes selfhood as well.[31] When someone defines a thing he or she tells us what it is. That is one gives its *māhīyya* or its whatness. But who can define Divinity? Who can find an expression (*ʿibāra*) that will capture the Divine Reality? Who can give a definition of Divinity?

We simply cannot present His *Hūwīyya*, the quality of His being He. We can never behold His dhāt, His *māhīyya* or essence (dhāt). All that is unknown (*majhūl*). Ordinary words, our *'ibārah*, fails to describe Him, at least, insofar as they are an expression of reason (*al-ʿaql*).

Now when the commentators discuss the grammatical role of "*hūwa*" in terms of a "pronoun of the fact"' (*ḍamīru 'sh-sha'n*) or "pronoun of the story (*ḍamīru 'l-qiṣṣah*) they are speaking on the level of *ʿilmu 'l-ʿibārah* as it was explained earlier. There is none. Thus most of the commentaries you will see stop after explaining the grammar of "*hūwa*." They do not continue because the Divine Essence is like a shoreless ocean. It is unbridgeable. We can never discern its shore even in the distance. It is beyond knowledge that can be expressed. According to Imām al-Ghazālī:

> That is why, when Pharaoh said to Mūsā, "And what is the Lord of the worlds?" (26:23) as if he was asking about the quality of being what He is, His What-ness or quiddity (*māhīyyatihi*), Mūsā answered by informing Pharaoh of Allāh's activities (*afʿāl*), since activities are the most manifest things in the questioner's eyes. Mūsā said "The Lord of the heavens and the earth" (26:24). Pharaoh said to those around him, "Did you not

[31] Among the Muslim philosophers, *dhāt* is sometimes used interchangeably with quiddity or whatness. Quiddity came into English from Latin as a translation of the Arabic *māhiya* which means the same as "whatness."

> hear?" (26:25) as if he was rebuking Mūsā for failing to answer his question touching upon Allāh's quiddity. Mūsā then said, "Your Lord and the Lord of your fathers, the ancients." (26:26) Thus, Pharaoh thought Mūsā was crazy, since he asked him what Allāh is like and what He is but was answered with acts. Hence, he said, "Surely, your messenger who was sent to you is mad! (26:27)

Pharaoh did not understand the difference between Allāh's Essence and His activities described by His Attributes.

Indeed, if all the world's oceans were ink and its trees pens, Allāh's Essence would remain indescribable. The ink and trees will disappear and end and the Divine, yet Knowledge will never end. Indeed, Allāh's names are endless. So what is our knowledge in the face of this reality? Our knowledge ends; it is limited. That is why Allāh's says:

وَفَوْقَ كُلِّ ذِي عِلْمٍ عَلِيمٌ

"Above every possessor of knowledge is the Owner of Knowledge (*fawqa kulli dhī''ilmin'Alīm*).

Al-'Alīm is, of course, Allāh Himself who is "The First, the Last, the Apparent and the Hidden ..." that is, "He is the absolute Knower of everything." How dare we then think that we have knowledge? We know, in fact, next to nothing.

In this light of this, we can understand the importance of what Sayyidunā 'Alī said concerning the meaning of "*Hūwa*." He relates:

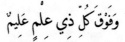

وحدثني أبي عن أبيه عن أمير المؤمنين (ع) أنه قال رأيت الخضر في المنام

قبل بدر بليلة فقلت له علّمني شيئاً أنتصر به على الأعداء فقال قل يا

هو يا من لا هو إلا هو فلما أصبحت قصصت على رسول الله صلى

الله عليه وسلم فقال يا علي علمت الاسم الأعظم فكان على لساني يوم

بدر

I saw <u>Kh</u>iḍr whilst asleep (fī'l-manām) the night before the Battle of Badr. I said [to him]: "Teach me something by which I will emerge victorious over the enemy. He said [to me]: "Say: *Ya Hūwa man lā hūwa illa Hū!*"[O Who whom there is nothing except He] I thereupon went to relate what happened to the Messenger of Allāh ﷺ Then he said [to me]: "O 'Alī! You have been taught the greatest Name." Thus, it was on my tongue on the day of the Battle of Badr.[32]

He ﷺ told Sayyidunā 'Alī ؑ to say, *"Ya Hūwa man lā hūwa illā Hū!"* to have him affirm there is nothing existent save Allāh. For if there were in existence two things, then he would have used a dual pronoun to signify two things and not single out one. Instead, <u>Kh</u>iḍr judges that *mā siwā Allāh* —i.e., whatever is other than Allāh is totally non-existent. (*'adam maḥḍ*). Sayyidunā 'Alī ؑ says this in Battle because it is in the midst of conflict that we most need reminding of this.

---

[32] At-Tabrīzī (please check this name) in his *Bayān*.

So, in this story the Battle of Badr symbolizes every situation where there is conflict, situations in which the soul is most likely to lose its balance (i'tidāl). When this occurs, we must repeat as Sayyidunā 'Alī ☙ did: "Ya Hūwa man lā hūwa illa Hū!"

In order to clear away obscurities about the Divine Nature, Allāh orders Prophet Muḥammad ﷺ to say to the Arabs first "Hūwa," thereby evoking the Divine Essence, then to say "Allāh," to describe the most comprehensive of His names. In other words, Allāh shows us first that He is totally other than the world insofar as His Essence. Then He the Exalted gives his own proper name as "Allāh" to tell us that He is not other than the world insofar as His names and Attributes.

Thus, when the verse reveals the sounds and letters "Hūwa" the Arabs, the Jews and the Christians stood before the name of that Reality without the aspect of the Divine Names and Attributes. That is, they heard it and when it was written down, they saw the letters. They did not grasp the reality. For here, ordinary linguistic expression and cognition fail. For who can know the reality of His Essence?

No one can describe Him but Himself. If this were all that Allāh revealed, what the Arabs asked the Prophet ﷺ would not have been fully answered. So the revelation continues and they learn, "Hūwa Allāh." That is, when the idolaters approach Muḥammad and say to him,

صف لنا ربك

"ṣif lanā rabbaka!" (Describe to us your Lord)"

and

"Of what kind (jins) of thing is your Lord?" or more literally, "What genus is your Lord's supreme Reality?" He responds and shares with them His own name. As said, Allāh is a proper name, unlike "God." The latter is a general and descriptive term like *theos* in Greek. In contrast, Allāh refers uniquely to an individual.

Accordingly, the Arab grammarians say the *"lā"* in the formula of faith-testimony (*shahāda*) and unification (*tawḥīd*), *Lā ilaha illa 'l-Lāh* (There is no god but Allāh) is *"la li-nafi al-jins."* They mean the particle of negation "lā" takes in every member of the entire genus (*la nafiyatu 'l-jins*). The substitute (*al-badal*) following this denial is "Allāh." In other words, there is no category of things the idolaters call *"ilāh"* (pl.- *āliha*). Here, the semantic key is the Arabic definite article *"al"* or "the." It ensures that the reference of *al-Lāh* is to a reality and not simply a name. For the worship of the idolaters is caught up in a web of names. That is, they are the names they have invented to describe the power and forces they see at work in nature. They did not consider the ultimate source of power in the universe.

Nevertheless, in response to their request, the name Allāh was revealed. It is the name by which the Divine Reality names Himself in respect of being a speaker (*mutakallim*). For Allāh describes Himself by speech. In this respect, He stands in contrast to the divinities worshipped by the idolaters.

قَالُوا أَأَنتَ فَعَلْتَ هَذَا بِآلِهَتِنَا يَا إِبْرَاهِيمُ قَالَ بَلْ فَعَلَهُ كَبِيرُهُمْ هَذَا فَاسْأَلُوهُمْ إِن كَانُوا يَنطِقُونَ فَرَجَعُوا إِلَى أَنفُسِهِمْ فَقَالُوا إِنَّكُمْ أَنتُمُ الظَّالِمُونَ ثُمَّ نُكِسُوا عَلَى رُؤُوسِهِمْ لَقَدْ عَلِمْتَ مَا هَؤُلَاء يَنطِقُونَ

Recall the story Allāh tells about the encounter of the Prophet Ibrāhīm ﷺ with the idolaters of his time (21: 62-65). These latter had come to him after he had destroyed their idols and asked: "Is it thou whom has done this to our gods, O Ibrāhīm?" And he said: "Question them [sc. the gods], if they can speak." To this, the idolaters cried out to Ibrāhīm ☼, "'Well thou knowest that these speak not." The idols, that is, are dumb; they neither see nor hear.

For this reason, Allāh declares:

$$\text{مَا تَعْبُدُونَ مِن دُونِهِ إِلَّا أَسْمَاءً سَمَّيْتُمُوهَا أَنتُمْ وَآبَآؤُكُم}$$

"Those whom ye worship beside Him are but
names that you have named, ye and your fathers."
(12:40)

That is, they are not the names that I, the Exalted, name Myself. To understand this point listen for a moment to Shaykh ʿAbdu 'l-Ghanī an-Nablusī:

> You should know that all these attributes by which Allāh the Exalted describes Himself, either in the Qur'ān or upon the tongue of His Messenger are realities (maʿānin) characterized through His sublime Essence by eternality without beginning as well as eternality without end inasmuch as they are not the same as His Essence and yet not other than His Essence. Likewise, each attribute amongst them is not the same as the other and not other than it.

The Names and Attributes, then, are not names that human beings have named the Divine Reality. They are the names He the Exalted has used to name Himself. And did not the Prophet ☼ say:

$$\text{فضل كلام الله على سائر الكلام كفضل الله على سائر خلقه}$$

"The superiority of the Speech of Allāh over other discourse is like His own superiority over His creatures (*faḍlu kalāmi 'l-Lāhi 'alā sa'iri 'l-kalāmi ka-faḍli 'l- Lāhi 'alā khalqihi*)? [33]

Not only this, when the name "Allāh" was revealed, the most comprehensive name (*ism*) and a sign (*'alam)* of the Divine Essence was divulged. For the name "Allāh" designates at the same time every name and attribute just as the Qur'ān declares:

وَلِلّٰهِ الْأَسْمَاءُ الْحُسْنَىٰ فَادْعُوهُ بِهَا

"To Allāh belongs the most beautiful Names. Invoke Him by them!" (7:180)

and,

قُلِ ادْعُوا اللّٰهَ أَوِ ادْعُوا الرَّحْمٰنَ أَيًّا مَا تَدْعُوا فَلَهُ الْأَسْمَاءُ الْحُسْنَىٰ

"Call upon Allāh or call upon the All-Merciful; by whichever name ye invoke Him, to Him belong the most beautiful Names." (17:110).

Thus, all the Beautiful Divine Names are included within the name Allāh.

This is easy to understand each Divine Name has both a sense and a reference. We speak of the evening star and the morning star but refer to the same thing. Only the meanings "evening star" and "morning star" differ. The two terms both refer to the same planet Venus. Similarly, all the Divine Names refer to the Divine Essence (*adh-Dhat*) as Shaykh 'Abdu 'l-Ghanī an-Nablusī indicated above. At the same time they display different meanings which, as he

[33] In at-Tirmidhī, Thawābu'l-Qur'ān 25; cf. al-Bukhārī, *Jāmi'u'ṣ-Ṣaḥīḥ*: Kitabu faḍā'il l- qur'ānī: Bāb faḍli' l-qur'āni' 'alā sā'iri'l-kalām, 1107.

also indicates, are nor simply distinct linguistic meanings. They represent different realities.

Explaining this, Shaykh Ismā'īl Haqqī al-Bursawī in his *Rūḥu 'l-Bayān* describes the three expressions (*alfā·*), "*Hūwa,*" "*Allāh,*" *Āḥad*" as follows:

قوله هو الله احد ثلاثة ألفاظ كل واحد منها اشارة الى مقام من مقامات السائرين الى الله تعالى فالمقام الاول مقام المقربين وهم الذين نظروا الى ماهيات الاشياء وحقائقها من حيث هى هى فلا جرم ما رأوا موجودا سوى الله

> Each of them [functions as] as an allusion (*ishārah*) to one of stations (*maqāmāt*) of the travellers on the path to Allāh the Exalted. The first is the station of those who draw near (*maqāmu 'l-muqarrabīn*). That is the meaning of "*Hūwa.*" They looked at everything and they did not see anything except Allāh. Everything they look at takes them to the reality of the Creator.

This is the level of the near ones in paradise, the *maqāmu 'l-muqarrabīn*. Those at this level look at the realities of everything in this *dunyā* as mere creatures but creatures that lead them immediately to their Creator. Submerged in the supersensible ocean of Divine Reality they can only cry, "*Ya Hūwa man lā hūwa illa Hū!*"

In the *Haqā'iqu 't-Tafsīr* of Abū 'Abdi-r-Raḥmān as-Sulamī the master Ibn 'Aṭā' is quoted as saying:

> There are two [kinds of] knowledge (*al-ma'rifatu ma'rifitān*). [The first] is knowledge of the Real (*al-*

> *Ḥaqq*). [The second] is knowledge of Reality (*al-ḥaqīqah*). As for knowledge of the Real (*al-Ḥaqq*) it is] knowledge of His Oneness according to the Names and Attributes He has manifested to humankind. As for knowledge of reality (*al-ḥaqīqah*), there exists no way to it inasmuch as the Divine Impenetrability and realization of Divine Lordship prevent it according to Allāh's statement: "With knowledge they comprehend Him not."() The verse means that there is no access to knowledge of the [Divine] Reality (*al-ḥaqīqah*).

That is, there is no access to the level of *Hāhūt* which is Divinity's own Infinite Self. We are restricted in our expressions (*'ibārāt*) about it because we are finite. No human life is long enough to list all the elements of anything approaching an adequate definition of the type the jurists (*fuqahā'*) employ when establishing legal analogy (*qiyās*), for example.

Each Divine Name, of course, signifies the reality of the Divine Essence. But it is that Essence considered from the standpoint of some relationship (*nisbah*) Allāh assumes with His creation. As reported earlier, "Everything has a relation and the relation to Allāh exists in *Sūratu 'l-Ikhlāṣ* To use the words of Shaykh Ismā'īl Haqqī al-Bursawī, commenting on *Sūratu 'l-Ikhlāṣ* in his well-known *tafsīr*, *Rūḥu 'l-Bayān*, "There exists a bond between oneness and creation namely, [the bond] between divinity and that for whom it is a divinity (*ilāhīyya wa-l-ma'lūhīyya*)."

Elaborating on the same point, the Naqshbandī Shaykh 'Abdu 'l-Ghanī an-Nablusī writes:

> All the [Divine] Attributes are but a relation between Allāh, the Exalted, and the world (*al-'alam*). The world did not emerge nothingness (*al-*

> ʿ*adam*) into existence (*al-wujūd*) out the Eternal [Divine] Essence except by the mediation of [that Essence] also describing Itself by these eternal Attributes.

"*Hūwa*" in contrast denotes Allāh as utterly transcendent and independent of His creatures. The Qur'ān says,

إِنَّ اللهَ لَغَنِيٌّ عَنِ الْعَالَمِينَ

"Allāh is altogether independent (Ghanī) of the worlds (29: 6)"

and,

يَا أَيُّهَا النَّاسُ أَنتُمُ الْفُقَرَاءُ إِلَى اللهِ وَاللهُ هُوَ الْغَنِيُّ الْحَمِيدُ

"O People! ye are needy in relation (*al-fuqarā'*) to Allāh and He is the Independent (*al-Ghanī*), the Owner of praise. (35:15)."

That is, as Essence He stands aloof to the cosmos. Viewed from this perspective the Divine Essence represents Absolute Hiddeness (*al-ghaybu' l-muṭlaq*). Except, when the name Allāh is revealed to the Prophet ﷺ it comes to Him with all its manifestations, the infinite Names of these manifestations and the infinite descriptions those names depict. Allāh dressed him with them and in them he stands eternally clad.

But God reveals still more about Himself. So, after Allāh, we read "*Āḥad*" placed it in grammatical opposition (*badal*) to Allāh. "*Āḥad*" is chosen because "*wāḥid*" or the numeral "one" in Arabic is used to count. It thus figures in enumerating things. For *wāḥid* joins to something else like it so they become two or to yet another thing so that they become three and so on. In this respect "*wāḥid*" differs from "*al-āḥad*" that does not allow a second to follow after it. It names that which is unique.

Allāh thereby informs us that His relation to His creation ultimately transcends all relations. He thus reveals Himself as the *ghaybun mutlaq* or the Absolutely Unseen, the Hidden Treasure. But since Allāh is loving, He is constrained by a love to reveal Himself. Such is the character of the Divine Love whose nature is to give of itself receives explanation in the famous sacred *ḥadith qudsī*[34],

كُنتُ كَنزاً لا أُعرَفُ فَأَحبَبتُ أَنْ أُعرَفَ، فَخَلَقتُ خَلقاً

> "I was a treasure unknown, then I wished to be known; thus I created creation that I might be known (*kuntu kanzan lā 'urafu, fa aḥbabtu an 'urifa fa-khalaqtu 'l-khalq).*"[35]

There is, because of the act of creation a certain restriction (*al-taqyīd)* on the Divine nature if one may speak this way. On that restriction as al-Bursawī writes,

> The restriction comes out of the nature of the Divine Names themselves. But it is a self-restriction that arises out of the logic of the situation of love, so to speak, that is, the situation of the Creator's love of His creation. For beauty (*al-Jamāl*) communicates itself by its very nature. And its in

[34] A *hadīth qudsī* is a statement whose meaning directly reflects the meaning God intended but whose linguistic expression is not His uncreated Divine speech as communicated in the Qur'ān. It thus differs from a *hadīth nabawī* or prophetical *hadīth* whose meaning and linguistic expression are those of the Prophet Muḥḥammad, even though they represent expressions of the Divine will and are to that degree part of the revelatory deposit known as the *Sunna*.

[35]

> the nature of light (*al-Nūr)*) to shine forth. Truth (*al-Ḥaqq*) cannot remain hidden but must manifest itself or it is not truth. And so if *al-Ḥaqq* is to reveal Himself, He must restrict Himself by the nature of the very properties He displays and He willing to do so because He Himself is Love (*al-Wadud*) and yearns to be known.

Yet, this restriction stems from the Divine love. We hear many Muslims rehearse the formula derived from the Qur'ān: "Allāh can do whatever He wants." And this is true. At the same time, would He be a loving or Merciful God, if a farmer planted corn and apples trees came up or a married couple planned for a baby and the mother gave birth to a lion cub? To say Allāh has simply promised that evil-doers are punished and good people are rewarded is not enough. It is because Allāh loves His creation that things operate according to their divinely given natures.

In this connection, it is important to know that al-Āḥad and al-Wāḥid are two different divine names. Al-Wāḥid describes the names and attributes. But Ahad refers to the Essence. Al-Āḥad is the actual Essence by itself (*al-Ahad Hūwa al-dhāt wahduha*). No description of the essence exists. We can only name it. It also allows us to know that the other names al-Karīm, ar-Ra'ūf, etc. describe that essence. That is, all these attributes point to al-Wāḥid and al-Wāḥid points to al-Āḥad.

Hence, the third level in the revelation of this *sūrah* passing from "Hūwa" and "Allāh" is al-Āḥad. "*Qul! Hūwa Allāh.*" was in reality enough for believers. But others did not believe, so Allāh added to the description "Āḥad." Āḥad tells the unbelievers "Don't go astray!" Allāh is *Āḥad* in all attributes, since each attribute is uniquely His own. Accordingly, Sayyīdunā Bilāl ﷺ used to say, "*Āḥad, Āḥad* and did not say, "Allāh, Allāh." There are those who make *dhikr* with *Hū* and those who make *dhikr* with Allāh and those who use the *taḥlīl* or *"lā ilāha illa-Llāh"* (There is no divinity save Allāh). Those who have reached a high level also use Allāh for *dhikr* since it takes in all the attributes.

While many names exist to describe the Divine reality that reality itself remains Unique — *Ahad.* Paraphrasing Ismāʿīl Ḥaqqi al-Bursawī, *al-Āḥad* is the name owned by the Unique with whom no partner exists to share anything vis-à-vis His essence (*wa-l Āḥad ismun li man la yushāriku fī dhātihi*) just as *al-Wāḥid* is the name owned by the Unique with whom no partner shares anything vis-à-vis His attributes (*al-Wāḥid li man la yushāriku fī sifātihi*). Al-Bursawī goes on to say:

ان الاحد هو الذات وحدها بلا اعتبار كثرة فيها فأثبت له الاحدية التى

هى الغنى عن كل ما عداه وذلك من حيث عينه وذاته من غير اعتبار

امر آخر والواحد هو الذات مع اعتبار كثرة الصفات وهى الحضرة

الاسمائية

> It means that *Āḥad* is the essence alone without any aspect of multiplicity (*bi-lā iʿtibāri kathrati*); for uniqueness (*Āḥadīyya*) is affirmed of Him, independent of whatever goes beyond it and that qua His identity and His essence as such without an aspect of another state of affairs; while oneness (wāḥid*iiya)* is the essence accompanied by the attributes, i.e., the presence of the names.

Qul! Hū Allāhu Āḥad (Say: He is Allāh the Unique) thus shows itself to be sufficient as an answer to the question posed by the *mushrikūn* (idolaters) who asked the Prophet "Describe to us your

Lord (*Sif/unsib lanā rabbaka*)." For it provided them knowledge that the proper object of human worship is the unique Divine Essence. It opens to them possibility of true *tawḥīd*. Monotheism is an abstract name in English is not a god translation for *tawḥīd*. In Arabic *tawḥīd,* as verbal noun, signfies an action, namely, the action of repeating on one's tongue the *kalimat at-tawḥīd*: *lā ilāha illa-Llāh*—There is no You know the Essence through His Names. So God described His Names only. Not His Divine Essence.

Again, in the words of Ismā'īl Ḥaqqi al-Bursawī commenting on *Sūratu-l-Ikhlāṣ* writes as follows:

لذا قال تعالى ان الهكم لواحد ولم يقل لأحد لان الواحدية من اسماء التقييد فبينهما وبين الخلق ارتباط اى من حيث الالهة والمألوهية بخلاف الاحدية اذلا يصح ارتباطها بشئ فقولهم العلم الالهى هو العلم بالحق من حيث الارتباط بينه وبين الخلق وانتشاء العالم منه بقدر الطاقة البشرية

> Thus, Allāh says [in the Holy Qur'ān, "*wa ilāhukum ilāhun Wāḥid.*" (Your God is One God) and did not say [*wa ilāhukum ilāhun*] *Āḥadun* (Your God is a unique God). For oneness (*wāḥidīyya*) insofar as the names are concerned represents restriction (*taqyīd*) inasmuch as a bond exists between oneness and creation, namely, [the bond] between divinity and that for whom it is a divinity (*ilāhīyya wa-l-ma'lūhīyya*). [Thus,] oneness differs from uniqueness since it is incorrect [to posit] a bond [between uniqueness] and anything [whatsoever]. [Hence, when scholars] speak of the "science of divinity" (*'ilm ilāhī*) [or theology] [they have in mind their] knowledge of ultimate reality

> according to that bond between divinity and the created order [or] the origin of the cosmos according to the measure of human capability and [only] to the extent that [such knowledge] does not cancel out that human capability.

The theologians of Islam, in other words, know that affirming the uniqueness (*tawḥīd*) of the Divine essence pertains to the real nature of Allāh, the Exalted as He is in Himself and not as He relates to His creatures. For every Divine name implies a relation (*nisba*) between God and His creation.

"Between oneness and creation there exists a bond" the above passage says," namely, [the bond] between divinity and that for whom it is a divinity (*ilāhīyya wa-l-ma'lūhīyya*)." For there is no All-Merciful One (*al-Raḥmān*) unless there is also some object of mercy (*al-marḥūm*), no Creator (*al-Khāliq*) unless there is a creature (*al-makhlūq)* and so on for all the Beautiful Names. From that name *Wāḥid,* creation appeared, because from that name *al-Qādir* appeared and creation resulted, not from the name *Āḥad*. *Āḥad* is beyond that. So *Wāḥid* expresses a relationship between human beings and Allāh who wants them to know Him. Hence, by that Name they know Him. That is where the relationship is built. To this end we are worshipping that object of worship as *al-Wāḥid*. *Al-Wāḥid* displays the relationship between Creator and created.

Hence, when the *mushrikūn* and the Jews of Khaybar ask: *unsib lanā rabbaka,* that is, "Make clear to us the relation of the your Lord to us," the Prophet was commanded to say: "*Hūwa Allāh*" and the pronoun "He" (*hūwa*) is the subject and "*Allāh*" is the predicate. He described the Names. He directed them first to the level of *wa ilāhukum ilāhun Wāḥid. Wāḥid*, i.e., "He your God is One God."

But *wa ilāhukum ilāhun Wāḥid,* that *Wāḥid* also signals a relationship between human beings, Allāh wants human beings to know Him. So through that Name they know Him. That is where the relationship is built. So you are worshipping that One to be worshipped, *al-Wāḥid*. So *Wāḥid* shows the relationship between Creator and created. *Āḥad* is complete unknown, you cannot understand it or reach it and no one can understand or share. This level one calls the *ḥaḍrah* (presence or dignity) of the Names and Attributes. Because Allāh longed to be known He revealed first His names: "There is no *ilāh* except Him, the Merciful, the Beneficent." That divine reality represents the *ḥaḍra* of *wāḥidīyya*.

$$\text{اللهُ الصَّمَدُ}$$

That is, "Allāh, the Self-Sufficient upon whom creatures depend." The subject (*al-mubtadi'*) is Allāh, the predicate (*al-khabar*) is *aṣ-Ṣamad*. It comes from the root Ṣ-M-D which can connote " to turn to" or "to need," "to set up," "to erect something, "to remain unchanged or unaffected," "to be sublime, everlasting." However, when *Sūratu 'l-Ikhlāṣ* was revealed, Ibn 'Abbās ؓ narrates, people asked: "What is *aṣ-Ṣamad*? The Prophet ﷺ said: "He is whom one turns to in needs." That is, because He alone is capable of fulfilling them. *Aṣ-Ṣamad* thus denotes an action (*fi'l*) in the sense of it being executable (*maf'ūl*) like one says, "grasp" and at the same time signifies something capable of grasping. Similarly, *aṣ-Ṣamad* means the one whom one turns in need as well as the One capable of being turned to in need. He does not stand in need of anything by His very Essence. In this sense *aṣ-Ṣamad* is *Āḥad* or Unique.

But the Qur'ān repeats that "Allāh is *aṣ-Ṣamad*" to affirm our dependence on Him and the exact character of Allāh's relation to us. By this it signifies that *aṣ-Ṣamad* is one of the names that describes the Creator's relation to His creatures. That is, it is one of names through which Allāh discloses Himself to people through His Divine *tajalliyāt*. Allāh manifests these *tajalliyāt* or disclosures of Himself in order to guide His creation. There are an infinite number of names. And all creatures are under the *tajallī* of one name or another at different times.

To the extent that ordinary people find themselves devoted to *dunyā* and not to *ākhira,* they are unable to carry Divine Disclosures. The Prophet Muḥammad ﷺ however, who came two bow lengths are less into the Divine presence, was able to carry all the *tajallīs* manifest there as we see in the narrations of *Laylat al-Isrā' wa 'l-Mi'rāj* — the Night Journey and Ascension. Since not everyone can carry all these *tajallīs,* one *walī* specialized in one, and another in another. This is a mercy for humankind. That is why there occurs differences between what the *ṣaḥāba* understood. And these differences color the ḥadīth they narrate. But the Prophet ﷺ is like a mainline carrying an entire community's water supply. Others carry what their capacity permits. According to your container's size, then, will Allāh disclose Himself.

Now 'Abdu'ṣ-Ṣamad or Servant of as-Ṣamad is where the quality of being dependent on Allāh is disclosed to the one who truly turns to Him, that is, to the one who aims to prevent affliction, bring about the support of good things and thus intercede to Allāh to ward off punishment and bestow reward. His is the place where Allāh looks to the world in His Lordship and he is the man through whom God watches and cares for this world. Through that place of disclosure (*maẓhar*) people receive their permission for provision (*rizq*). For the 'Abd aṣ-Ṣamad is able to guide people and creature to their sustenance There is one 'Abdu'ṣ-Ṣamad in every century. He is the unique owner of that name in that time just as there is every century there is a Servant of the One —'Abdu 'l-Wāḥid. One goes; another comes.

In a similar fashion does an 'Abdu 'l-Āḥad, —the Servant of the Unique come and go. It is important to note that under this Divine name (*ismu 'l-Lāh*) al-Āḥad, however, *al-quṭbīyyatu 'l-kubrā* or "*al-*

Quṭbu 'l-aʿẓam," appears. In Arabic the word "*quṭb*" means "axis" or "pole." He is the central figure in the hierarchy of saints. Implicit is the idea of the pole star which stands opposite above the Kaʿaba in Makka, the guiding light for pilgrims. Therefore, the word "pole" connotes an upward orientation. Thus, it is associated with the *Laylat al-Isrā' wa 'l-Miʿrāj* since in the Muslim symbolism of space the point of orientation of the soul is up into the heights of Divine glory. This does not exclude piercing into the depths of Divine reality, however. That is why the Prophet ﷺ said, "Make no invidious comparison between me and Yūnus ibn Mattā because my journey is into the heights and his into the depths."[36] There are then two ways to reach the Divine: the journey upward into the heavens and the journey inward into the depths of Mercy's oceans.

In any case, the ʿAbdu 'l-Āḥad, the one whom we call "the greatest pole or *quṭb* in this world (*dunyā*), holds sway over all other *aqṭāb: Quṭb, quṭb al-bilad, quṭb al-irshād, quṭbu 't-tasarruf, quṭbu 'l-aqṭāb*. The *quṭb al-aqṭāb* directs these *quṭbs*. Also, for this reason he is called *Sulṭānu 'l-awliyā'*, Sultan of the saints. Our master Shaykh ʿAbd Allāh Fā'iz ad-Daghestānī was *Sulṭānu 'l-awliyā* in his time and our master Shaykh Nāẓim ʿAdil al-Ḥaqqānī bears that title today.

As said earlier, this world of *al-mulk* "parallels the world of *malakūt*" so that "there is nothing in the former that is not a representation (*mithāl*) for something in the latter." In other words, each being in *mulk* has its own *malakūt* that is its cause that contains and encloses it. This is its inner, secret or archetypal reality that at the same time acts as its watchman and guardian. Even the Kaʿaba with its four walls, represents something beyond

36

what ordinary people see with the physical eye. For to ordinary vision there is simply a procession around it. To those whose gaze extends beyond the world of *mulk*, there is more, since the earthly Kaʿaba earth is but a reflection of the *Bayt al-Maʿmūr* (the much frequented house) in heavens. It is the inner secret or heavenly reality of the earthly Kaʿaba and exercises guardianship over it through the agency of the ranks of *aqṭāb* just mentioned.

So whenever one faces the four walls of the Kaʿaba one in reality faces these *aqṭāb* if you have eyes to see. If so, you do not see the Kaʿaba's black stone except you see the *walī* guardian of that stone as well. He is the fifth of those *aqṭāb* whom the enlightened pilgrim faces as he or she approaches the sides of the Kaʿaba. That is why Sayyidunā ʿAlī ﷺ reproved Sayyidunā ʿUmar ﷺ for saying "I kiss that stone as following the Prophet ﷺ because I see it does not harm you or give benefit." And Sayyidunā ʿAlī exclaimed, "What are you saying? That is going to bear testimony (*shahāda*) in your behalf on Judgment Day."

Our master Grand Shaykh ʿAbd Allāh Fā'iz ad-Daghestānī, experienced one vision in which he was shown the *walī* behind the stone when he kissed it. In this way, a spiritual element entered his veneration of the stone which dematerialized it and transformed the Kaʿaba's stone into a temple of faith. That came about, not through the stone nor through the sides of the Kaʿaba. A light shining from beyond takes over Kaʿaba's material form. It is not in the light. Rather, it *is* the light itself. The Divine act of illumination energizes human experience and turns it inside out, so to speak, like a glove is turned inside out so that its inside becomes the enveloping surface.

لَمْ يَلِدْ وَلَمْ يُولَدْ

That is, "Who did not beget nor was begotten." This verse comes as a response to those who claimed that the angels are Allāh's children or those who claimed that Sayyidunā ʿĪsā 🕊 is his son, or those who said that He took Sayyidunā ʿĪsā 🕊 as a son. For there were some Christians who claimed that ʿĪsā 🕊 was in his very being God's son from the beginning of his life. Other Christians said that God took him as his son at a certain point in his earthly career by adoption, as it were. Thus, the oft repeated phrase that Allāh "had not taken a son" —*māʾttakhadha walada.* Here, in this verse Allāh answers the former group with the words *"lām yalid"* "he did not beget" in the past tense.

In revealing this verse to the Prophet 🕊 Allāh is saying to those who claimed that some time in the past Allāh took ʿĪsā as a son, that He never had a son. For begetting children would count against His Lordship or *Rubūbīyya* inasmuch as it negates His Divine Attributes. If we say *walad,* a child, he is going to take the characteristics of his father, his mother, his parents. The child is a human being. If Allāh has a child, that child is going to be a god also, and that never ends. Accordingly, this verse negates child bearing or offspring to Allāh. "Tell them, O Muhammad," it says, "this is incorrect, and inform them He is not in need of having a child in the past, *lām yalid,* and in fact, Allāh never had a child." Again the *al-māḍī* form or past tense is used and means Allāh was not born nor will He ever be born from someone else.

Consider this verse and how it proclaims the difference between the servant and the Creator. The servant pursues pleasure. And by doing so acts according to the way Allāh made us. He fashioned us to be in need of such things. We must marry, for example. Yet, Allāh is different. He has no need for a female companion or *ṣāḥiba* as He Himself declares in *Sūratu 'l-Anʿām*: "Originator of the heavens and earth! How can He have a child, when there is for

Him no consort, when He has created all things and is of all things the Knower?

بَدِيعُ السَّمَاوَاتِ وَالأَرْضِ أَنَّى يَكُونُ لَهُ وَلَدٌ وَلَمْ تَكُن لَّهُ صَاحِبَةٌ وَخَلَقَ كُلَّ شَيْءٍ وهُوَ بِكُلِّ شَيْءٍ عَلِيمٌ

—badī'u 's-samawāti wa 'l-arḍi annā yakūn lahu waladun wa lām takun lahu ṣāḥibatun wa khalaqa kulla shay'in wa hūwa bi kulli shay'in 'alīm

—the Originator of the heavens and the earth! How could it be that He should have a child without there ever having been a mate for Him - since it is He who has created everything, and He alone knows everything? (6:101)

And He repeats the same thing again in *Sūrat Jinn*:

مَا اتَّخَذَ صَاحِبَةً وَلَا وَلَدًا

mā'ttakhadha ṣāḥibatan wa lā walada.
"He never took a female companion nor a son" (72:3)

But since He never begets nor was begotten He is not in any way like anyone else. The present verse thus echoes the complete negation of all human characteristics of Divinity found in the Qur'ān. As Allāh says: "There is nothing like unto Him …*laysa ka-mithlihi shay'un.* That is, it is impossible to relate any creaturely characteristics to the Divine Essence.

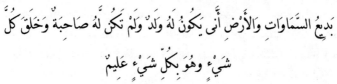

At the same time, Allāh continues the verse and declares: "and He is the all-Hearing the all-Seeing "— *wa hūwa's-samī'u 'l-basīr.* That is, Allāh simultaneously describes two ways in which He relates Himself to creatures. He hears whatever you say, even what comes to your heart so that we must be careful even of what comes to our hearts. Allāh monitors where we go and sees what we do and hears what we say. Allāh can not only hear your voice, but hears what your heart is saying and He hears the blood of the body saying "Allāh" or saying something else. That is why in *Sūratu 'l-Qāf* He says:

وَنَحْنُ أَقْرَبُ إِلَيْهِ مِنْ حَبْلِ الْوَرِيدِ

wa naḥnu aqrabu min ḥabli 'l-warīd.
"We are nearer to him than the jugular vein" —
(50:16)

That is, "and not anyone is equal to Him." Allāh's intention here is to negate anyone's being equal to His Divine Essence. No one equals Him, like no one is like Him (*lām yumāthilhu*) nor does anyone resemble Him (*lām yushākilhu*). After all, Allāh is the Creator of the very idea of equality. And if it were not for Him there would be no instances of things being equal.

In the final analysis we must note how every verse or *āya* of this *sūra* is a *tafsīr* or commentary of the *āya* before it. When they asked, "Who is He (*hūwa*)?" the answer comes in the *tafsīr*, "Āḥad." And when it is asked, "Who is Āḥad?" the *tafsīr* is, aṣ-Ṣamad. When they ask, "Who is aṣ-Ṣamad" the gloss appears "He who did not beget nor was begotten." Then when the question comes "Who is He who did not beget nor was begotten?" The *tafsīr* is "the One to whom no one is equal."

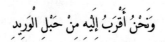

6

The Science of the Letters

Now the scholars of Islam are agreed that the understanding of certain matters comes only from Allāh and corresponds to the station (*maqām*) of the servant in the Divine Presence. This pertains especially to the letters making up the words of the Qur'ān. After all, Allāh revealed to the Prophet ﷺ twelve thousand oceans of knowledge. These twelve thousand oceans constitute the reality of each letter in the Qur'ān. We ought then not to find it strange when scholars bring out of a given word or letter of the Qur'ān numerous meanings. Therefore, when it comes to the letters that make up the words of the Qur'ān scholars agree that a single letter having one apparent meaning in the grammar of the language can be understood to have countless other meanings and numerous marvels. This is all from the bounty of the All-Merciful One who loses no opportunity to draw His servants to Himself even by means of the humblest things of His creation.

If this is true in humble things, how much more is it true with the noble letters of the Qur'ān in general and in *Sūratu 'l-Ikhlāṣ* in particular. In them, Allāh has placed special benefits available to servants who strive to draw close to him in meditation and prayer. Imām Ja'far aṣ-Ṣādiq[37] an early link in that Golden Chain mentioned earlier explains why this is so.

[37] He was the son of Imām Muḥammad al-Bāqir, son of Imām Zayn al-'Abidīn ff the son of the Prophet's cousin and husband of his daughter Fāṭima ff, 'Alī ibn Abī Ṭālib ff. But his mother was the daughter of al-Qāsim whose grandfather was Ja'far whose grandfather was Abū Bakr aṣ-Ṣiddīq.

> When Allāh thought about something, intended it and willed it, the objects of His thought, will and intention were the letters (*al-ḥurūf*). He made [a letter] the root (*aṣl*) of each thing, the sign signifying each perceptible object and the cutting edge of each thing fashioned. It is from these letters that everything is known: the name "true," the name "false," the action, the agent, the object of action, the meaningful and the meaningless. [The letters] sum up everything].

Some background concerning the origin of the world as told both in modern and traditional science will be of help in understanding this brief passage.

An earlier book, The Approach of Armageddon, described how most cosmologists today believe that all matter in its essence and origin is light. Their theory does not contradict aḥādīth passed down by Muslims through the ages. As said, these traditions tell us how the Prophet was the first thing Allāh created from His light. They describe how this light dwelt before Him, turning in the midst of His Divine Power. Allāh directed His gaze towards that light seventy times each day and each night, adding a new light with each glance and thus increasing its intensity of until at last the accumulated thermonuclear heat erupted in a vast primordial explosion creating our universe.

In other words, deep in the burning hearts of massive stars, the vital elements of life, as well as the heavy metals were manufactured. These stars, dying in supernova explosions, blasted out their stellar matter and distributed it in interstellar space, prior to its being recycled into suns, moons, and planets. We ourselves and indeed all life on earth are only possible because of the carbon and mineral formations forged in the light energy of stars that died in explosions billions of years ago.

An important piece of scientific evidence for the idea that the universe began in the way these scientists describe is a steady stream of microwave radiation permeating the atmosphere of our earth from outer space. Apparently, it is an echo of that initial explosion that scientist call the "Big Bang." It reverberates right up to present moment around our universe even though billions of years have elapsed since that event. All this means that formation of the galaxies was attended by intense sonic booms, suggesting an intimate connection between sound and light. Like twin flames, where one is the other is there as well. Sound lays down an underlying carpet of vibration, organizing clouds of intergalactic dust into nodes and eddies that began to form vast clusters of stars.

A more familiar example of how this happens is the energy that attends the phenomenon of resonance. Resonance is the force that causes bridges to collapse when armies walk across in unison, or shatters a glass when a singer reaches a certain note, or causes every pendulum clock in a given room to swing in unison. But this means that when the vibrations of sound vibrate in resonance, we have the capacity to transform the world around us. In fact, according to quantum string theory, each elementary particle is composed of a single string-that is, each particle is a single string - and all strings are absolutely identical.

Differences between particles arise because their respective strings undergo different resonant vibrational patterns that appear to be different elementary particles are actually different "notes" on a fundamental string. The universe-being composed of an enormous number of these vibrating strings-is akin to a cosmic symphony." Long ago the traditional sciences of Islam, of course, uncovered this hidden power of sound, and especially of resonance. However, they used it not only to transform the world around us but also the world of our inner selves.

The insight of the *awliyā'u 'l-Lāh* then is this. "When we read the Qur'ān aloud or repeatedly vocalize the names of Allāh we tap into the sound vibrations that sustain the universe. For every sound has a corresponding visible shape or pattern in the form of a Qur'ānic letter. This applies to the segmented letters in the Qur'ān beginning various sūrahs as well as those forming its individual words and sentences. The Qur'ān in this way holds the key to shaping our inner world, not according to our own whims and desires but according to the laws of resonance governing the universe' They are neither something dreamed up or invented by the human mind, nor something apprehended by it, at least, not in their essential reality. Rather, they are signatures of a rhythm beat out and heard by a heart in harmony with the creative forces of the universe.

Allāh placed Himself in the Qur'ān. In no other previous scripture does He place Himself in the way He places Himself in Qur'ān. For no other revelation can claim to be His own uncreated speech. What greater consolation could a servant want than this? When a person reads the Qur'ān in tones identical to those that Prophet ﷺ revealed, does it make sense to claim that Allāh is going to punish him or her? Will He send a tongue, charged with the same sonic energies that produced the event of the Qur'ān's revelation to hell? It is unimaginable! The uncreated sonic energies vibrating through the air each time the Qur'ān is recited thus count as evidence of Divine Mercy and justifies Allāh description of the Prophet when He says:

وَمَا أَرْسَلْنَاكَ إِلَّا رَحْمَةً لِّلْعَالَمِينَ

mā arsalnāka illā Raḥmatan li-l-'ālamīn

We have only sent you to the worlds as a mercy
(21:107)

This mercy characterizes the Prophet's function as messenger and communicator (*muballigh*).

The shapes of letters making up the Qur'ān then represent patterns of varying cosmic sound frequencies existing since the creation of the world. As Imām Jaʿfar aṣ-Ṣādiq has told us, Allāh "made [a letter] the root of each thing, the sign [signifying] each perceptible object and the cutting edge of each thing fashioned." For "*ḥarf*" the word for letter in Arabic means "edge." And they are in their own way like the edges we find on a sword or a knife. Just as the edge of a surgeon's knife may be-used to heal us, the letters of the Qur'ān hold the secrets to our health and well-being. They cut the chains (*asbāb*) that tie us to *dunyā* and cause so many imbalances within our souls, anxiety, depression, dispiritedness, and langor. That is why Qur'ān itself declares,

أَلَا بِذِكْرِ اللهِ تَطْمَئِنُّ الْقُلُوبُ

"Surely, doth tranquility of hearts reside in the
vocal remembrance of Allāh (*dhikri 'l-Lah*)."(13:28)

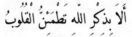

So, while these sacred letters help us to articulate the sounds that make up individual Arabic words they simultaneously symbolize different patterns of Divinely-created cosmic energy. This knowledge the Prophet took from Allāh, and passed on to Abū Bakr. It came not by acquisition (*kasb*) For the Prophet' ﷺ said, "What Allāh hath poured into my heart, I poured into the heart of Abū Bakr aṣ-Ṣiddīq. The jug into which one pours water does not acquire the water except perhaps in some metaphorical fashion, since the jug has neither will nor intention. With regard to the pouring of the contents of his heart the jug exercises no control anymore than did Abū Bakr aṣ-Ṣiddīq. The Prophet ﷺ poured the contents of his heart into Abū Bakr's heart.

But imagine the realities witnessed by the Prophet. These are thing of which not even angels have knowledge. Among these realities was the science of the letters (ʿilmu 'l-ḥurūf). Allāh had deposited these letters with the Prophet ﷺ at a moment that encompassed no angel drawing near to Him nor prophet whom He sent. In one such moment, as we have already learned, Allāh was directing His gaze towards the light of Muḥammad seventy times each day and each night, adding a new light with each glance and thus increasing its intensity. During this time, the transfer of energy was too intense and concentrated to allow any letter to be formed. This is why the Prophet ﷺ in his essential nature is unlettered and we call him "an-nabīyi 'l-ummī." He is prior to the letters just as he is prior to the pen (al-qalam) and all else, Again, recall the words of the ḥadīth quoted earlier where the Prophet ,

أول ما خلق الله نورُ نبيك يا جابر... ولم يكن في ذلك الوقت لوح ولا قلم ولا جنة ولا نار ولا ملك ولا سماء ولا أرض

> "O Jābir, the first thing Allāh created was the light of your Prophet from His light . . . and there was not, at that time, a Tablet or a Pen or a Paradise or a Fire or an angel or a heaven or an earth."[38]

Furthermore, we know from a narration concerning the revelation of the segmented letters kāf, hā' Yā', ʿain, ṣād that begin Sūrat Maryam that not even Jibrīl was informed such realities.

---

[38] 'Abd-Razzāq from Jābir ☘.

> When [the angel] Jibril, said *kāf,* the Prophet said "I know" (*'araftu*).Then he said "*hā*"', the Prophet said "I know." When he said "*yā*"' the Prophet said "I know." 'When Jibril said, "*'ayn,*" again the Prophet said "I know." [Finally] he said "*ṣāḍ*" and the Prophet said, "I know." Then Jibrīl asked, "How is it that you know what I know not?"[39]

This report then alerts us to the fact that Allāh deposited with the Prophet a knowledge that he has bestowed on no other creature.

From this order of knowledge everyone is excluded except the Prophet ﷺ. It touches on the secrets of the Qur'ān insofar as these pertain to the inner core of its essential reality. It also includes knowledge of the realities of the Divine Names and Attributes which no one knows but he ﷺ. No one but the Prophet ﷺ has divine permission to speak about this first kind of knowledge in any way.

The second kind of knowledge contains secrets of the Qur'ān about which the Prophet ﷺ is informed. This knowledge is peculiar to him and by right he alone can speaks of it. Still, others to whom permission has been granted may speak of things touching it. The third type of knowledge consists of things Allāh taught the Prophet ﷺ concerning both the clear and hidden meanings that He the Exalted deposited in His book and commanded the Prophet to divulge. This knowledge or science pertains to every aspect of the Qur'ān, the letters as well as the dots under the letters. We will only be able to reveal here a small part of this knowledge. But let us begin with the letters composing "Hūwa," *hā'* and *wāw* coming after the command "*qul*" and then move on to the letters making up "Allāh."

39

Secrets of Hā' *and* Wāw

Now according to Abū'l-'Abbās Ibn 'Aṭā', when in *Sūratu 'l-Ikhlāṣ* we read "*qul*" or "Say!" that command means:

> Make manifest what we have revealed and explained to you [O Muḥammad] by putting letters together. The letter "*hā'*" is a *ḥarfu-'t-tanbīh* [alerting us] to a fixed and stable meaning (*ma'nā thābit*) and the *wāw.'* is an allusion (*ishārah*) to those realities whose properties (*nu'ūt*) and attributes (*ṣifāt*) cannot be grasped by the senses (*bi 'l-ḥawass*).

Following "*qūl*," we find the *hā'* in "*hūwa*." According to the Arab grammarians when taken by itself simply as a letter, call *hā'* may function as a "*ḥarfu-'t-tanbīh*" a letter or rather particle that focuses attention on something in the immediate vicinity of the speaker. Hence, whatever it is to which the *hā'* excites our attention has to be near to us.

But in this case, what is near is "*hūwa*" the name of the Divine Essence. That Divine Reality is always here, it is always now. Has not Allāh said:

وَهُوَ مَعَكُمْ أَيْنَ مَا كُنتُمْ

"He is with you wherever you are" (57:4)

and

وَإِذَا سَأَلَكَ عِبَادِي عَنِّي فَإِنِّي قَرِيبٌ

"'When My servants ask about Me, then surely am I near." (2:186)

Hā' then is an *ishārah* to a fixed and stable reality (*ma'nā thābit*), namely the Divine Names and Attributes, as Ibn 'Ata' has informed us.

Thus, *Hā'* not only alerts that Allāh is present and near to whoever utters "*Hūwa.*" It also alerts us that He the Exalted is present in His sublime Names and Attributes. Then the *wāw* that immediately follows the *hā'*, Abū'l-ʿAbbās Ibn ʿAṭā' says is an *ishārah* or allusion. So after we are informed that He, the Exalted is near the *wāw* closing off the word "hūwa" reminds us that the properties (*nuʿūt*) and attributes (*ṣifāt*) it encloses are not to be grasped by the senses (*bi 'l-ḥawāss*),' *Ha'* and *wāw* as they appear in Hūwa then are flashpoints of eternal truth communicated by the Prophet from his super-sensuous contact with the realm of the unseen (*al-ghayb*). The letters of "*Hūwa*" appeared vibrating out of the infinite into the heart of Allāh's Messenger as tokens of his station in the Divine Presence.

Clearly, the letter *wāw* here in *Sūratu 'l-Ikhlāṣ* functions differently from the *wāw* used in swearing oaths, for example. And it is instructive to pause for a moment to understand why this is true, why, that is, Abū'l-ʿAbbās Ibn ʿAṭā' calls the *wāw* in "*Hūwa*" an *ishārah*. Commenting on the second verse of *Sūratu 'z-Zukhruf* (43:2): *wa 'l-kitābi 'l-mubīn* (By the Book which maketh plain).

The great *mufassir* Bayḍāwī writes, "Perhaps Allāh's swearing of an oath by certain objects is a mode of seeking testimony or proof on the basis of the evidence (*dalālah*) that those objects furnish for the thing sworn to (*al-muqsam ʿalayhi*)." Here, where *wāw* signifies "Allāh's proof for the child of Adam" to use the Prophet's words cited earlier. Bayḍawi describes the function of *wāw* as an *ʿibārah.* The latter facilitates our understanding of something in terms of something else as stated earlier.

Wāwu 'l-qasam, is an example of this because it denotes accompaniment (*maʿīyah*) or the joining of one thing to another (*ḍammu 'l-shay'i bi 'l-shay'*) in this case, the object sworn by (*muqsam bihi*). It thereby signifies the limitation attached to any proof (*ḥujjah*) or piece of reasoning (*ʿaql*) For swearing an oath by a person or a thing facilitates the understanding of the thing sworn in terms of the thing sworn by. For this reason, the object sworn by (*muqsam bihi*) usually consists of something perceptible to the five senses and is shareable by everyone endowed with the capacity to perceive by means of the senses.

Arguments of reason (*ʿaql*) often base themselves upon sense-experiences. Thus, sense experience often functions as evidence even in a proof (*ḥujjah* or *burhān*). Hence, often when *wawu 'l-qasm* is used the persuasiveness it evokes depends on "the evidence (*dalālah*) that those objects furnish for the thing sworn to (*al-muqsam ʿalayhi*)."

In this verse, the *wāw* in "*hūwa,*" however, is not meaningful in any persuasive or even descriptive sense. Instead functions therefore as an *ishārah* an allusion That is, *wāw* here does not participate in the reporting of something in terms of something else as in *wawu 'l-qasm*. Rather, it alludes directly to a reality which Allāh has unveiled as a sign (*ayah*) of His presence to His servant in an act of direct witnessing or *mushāhadah.* According to Abū'l-ʿAbbās Ibn ʿAṭā' this can happen because, "He is He (*hūwa hūwa*) and no one is able to report about the reality of His 'of the quality of being He (*huwīyya*) other than Himself." His comment continues:

> No one possesses an expression (*ʿibārah*) for Him with respect to Reality except He [who alone] has it of Himself. For He gives a report about Himself by means of the realness of His reality. Others report about Him according to the limit of His permission and command. But He reports of Himself that He is Allāh. He points (*ashāra*) from Himself to Himself inasmuch as no one has the right to point to Him other than He. 'Whoever points to Him, only points

> to His allusion (*is͟hārah*) to Himself. And for whoever makes an *is͟hārah* (allusion) that is genuine its genuineness is due to Divine glorification and protection. That person's *is͟hārah* is sound coinciding with the limits of [his] rectitude. But the person whose *is͟hārah* carries the air of pretended claim (*ad-daʿwa*) [his *is͟hārah*] it is invalid and far removed from the abode of reality (*al-ḥaqīqah*).

The *wāw* in *hūwa* then serves as an *is͟hārah* of the Divine Reality pointing to the Divine Reality. This means that letters making up "*Hūwa*" cannot be products of mere reason (*ʿaql*). Imām Husayn ibn ʿAlī was once heard to pray on Mount Arafat:

> [O Allāh!] How could an argument be given for Thine Existence by a being whose total and complete existence stands in need of Thee? When didst Thou ever disappear so that Thou mightest need evidence and logic to lead [minds] to Thee? And when didst Thou ever become far and remote so that Thy signs and effects made the people get in touch with Thee? Blind be the eye that seest Thee not, whilst Thou observest that [very] eye. 'What didst the one who missed Thee find? And what doth the one who findeth Thee lack? Surely, whoever delightest in or inclineth himself to other than Thee hath come to naught.

So, when a servant or handmaid of Allāh calls our attention to an *is͟hārah* in the Qur'ān or, indeed, in ourselves or in the horizon's of Allāh's creation he or she is only pointing to Allāh's own *ishārah* to Himself. Their *ishārah* is genuine because they stand under Divine Protection. That is, the *ishārah* is genuine only if he or she inhabits the station (*maqām*) of absolute Divine Selfhood (*huwīyya muṭlaqah*).

As said earlier, this is the station of those who are drawn near to the Divine Presence (*maqāmu 'l-muqarrabīn*). Those at this station look at everything and see nothing but Allāh. In other words, everything they look at takes them to the reality of their Creator. This is why Allāh promised them:

سَنُرِيهِمْ آيَاتِنَا فِي الْآفَاقِ وَفِي أَنفُسِهِمْ حَتَّى يَتَبَيَّنَ لَهُمْ أَنَّهُ الْحَقُّ أَوَلَمْ يَكْفِ
بِرَبِّكَ أَنَّهُ عَلَى كُلِّ شَيْءٍ شَهِيدٌ

"'We shall show them Our signs on the horizons
and within themselves, until it be manifest to them
that He is the Reality Doth not thy Lord suffice,
since He is 'Witness over all things." (41:53)

Now *wāw* is sounded through the two lips, the first place of articulation (*Āwwal u 'l-makhārij*). In a similar way, the sound *hā* is produced in the back of the throat (*al-ḥalaq*), the last place of articulation (*akharu 'l-makhārij*). For this reason, the third verse of *Sūratu 'l-Ḥadīd* is:

هُوَ الْأَوَّلُ وَالْآخِرُ

"Hūwa 'l-Āwwalu wa 'l-Akhiru"
—"He is the First and the last"

- and not *"Allāhu 'l-Āwwalu wa 'l-Akhiru"* — "Allāh is the First and the Last." Thus, the revelation of *Sūratu 'l-Ikhlāṣ* stands as a witness to the fact that of the Prophet ﷺ being clothed with the attributes the First and the Last. And it is the reason why he ﷺ said, "Allāh gave me knowledge of *Āwwalīn wa 'l-Akhirīn* – the Firsts and the Lasts." These are the *tajalīyāt* or disclosures of the Divine Reality to him ﷺ. Between *alif* and *hā'*, the Divine

Hiddenness and the *ākhirah,* that is, between the beginning and end, the treasury encompassing all the Beautiful Divine Names then reveals itself.

Secrets of Alif, Lām and Hā'

When the name Allāh is revealed to the Prophet ﷺ it comes to him with all its manifestations, the infinite names of these manifestations and the infinite descriptions those names depict. Allāh dresses the Prophet Muḥammad in each of them. So the letter in the name Allāh display and a comprehensiveness worthy of its status as the chief Divine Name. When we read its letters *Alif* and *lām* we summon forth the presence of the whole of life and reality. The one invoking the name Allāh thus travels on a journey starting with the *alif* passing to *lām* and ending up again with *hā'* or *Hu,* the name of the Divine Essence. That is, those meditating on this name within their hearts proceed then in a circle. They thus remind themselves that God is the First and the Last, the place of origin (*mabdā'*) and place of return (*ma'ād*).

But there is more. First, consider the presence of *"al"* — the definite article, before every Divine Name. It means that all of them actually begin with *alif.* This is a token of Allāh ennobling this letter in a special way as we learn from a report from 'Abd Allāh ibn Mas'ūd:

> All twenty-nine letters of the alphabet were displayed to the All-Merciful One. Then He [the Exalted] humbled the *alif* [by causing it no longer to stand upright. [But The *alif*] thanked Allāh for His humbling it. When it thanked Allāh He caused [the *alif*] to stand upright and made it the key to every name of His [Beautiful Names].

Now the definite article as we know comes before all the Divine names. This means that all begin with the letter *alif.* The *alif* serves then as a key first because prefixing the definite article before each name enables them to function as names of God.

In order to invoke effectively the unique Divine Cause of our sustenance, for example, we do not say *razzāq*. For without the definite article preceding it, we have only "*razzāq*" and "*razzāq*" by itself does not refer to the Divine Reality. The same is true of *ar-Raḥmān, ar-Raḥīm, al-Malik, al-Quddūs, as-Salām, al-Mu'min,* etc. With "*al*" attached, we truly pray to Allāh and can hope to be heard when we invoke Him. Dropping the definite article would be like saying "*ilāh*" instead of Allāh.

But we have learned that an *ilāh* is not Allāh. So, if you take away the *alif* in "*al*" you no longer have the name Allāh, the Name that signifies the proper object of worship (*al-ma'būd*). You have what "*mā siw'-Allāh,*" that is, what is other than Allāh. Thus, each time we mention on our tongues Allāh the *alif* in the definite article a we are reminded that without Allāh, the creation cannot exist.

But remove the *alif* from "Allāh" and there remains the letters - *lām, lām, hā'*. 'What remains is the Arabic preposition "*lām*" pointed with a *kasra* to indicate the vowel "i" underneath so that we read "*li.*" The Arab grammarians inform us that this preposition has several uses. Sometimes it signifies possession it is used to indicate someone's right of property or to show that something ascribed to a person is his or her own, or to show that a person has a right to it.

But the first *lām* is dropped, then we are left with *lahu* — "to Him." It thus indicates Allāh's right of possession over each of us. The *lām* joined to the pronoun "*hūwa*" in its shortened form shows that all thing are ascribed to Him as His own. This means that He has a right to us. For we own neither ourselves nor anything else in this *dunyā*, that is, the present world; nor in the world to come. The Qur'ān reminds us that: *"li 'l-Lāhi mā fī 's-samawāt wa mā fī 'l-arḍ"* —To Allāh belongs the Heavens and the Earth."[40] And it is also why it says,

يَا أَيُّهَا النَّاسُ أَنتُمُ الْفُقَرَاء إِلَى اللَّه

Ya hayuha'n-nāsu! antumu 'l-fuqarā'u ilā'l-Lāh
"O People! You are poor in relation to Allāh"

that is, "you are in need of Him." In this spirit Rabiʿa used to pray:

> O God! If I worship Thee for fear of Hell, burn me in Hell, and if I worship Thee in hope of Paradise, exclude me from Paradise; but if worship Thee for Thy own sake begrudge me not Thy everlasting beauty.

However, the grammarians also tell us that the letter *"lām"* expresses the purpose for which and the reason why anything is done. Thus, *"lahu"* can also mean "for Him" or "for His sake," that is, *"li 'l-Lāh"* —"for the sake of Allāh." The letters of the sacred name Allāh, when truncated in this fashion, signify that the entire creation exists for His sake and for the purpose for which He has made it. Has not Allāh said elsewhere:

وَمَا خَلَقْتُ الْجِنَّ وَالْإِنسَ إِلَّا لِيَعْبُدُونِ

mā khaqtu 'l-jinna wa 'l-insa illa li-yaʿbudūn

"I not created the jinn and humankind except to worship Me" (51:56)

[40] 2:284.

The commentary of Fāṭima an-Nisabūrī on this verse recorded in Sulamī's *Ḥaqā'iqu 't-Tafsīr* reads:

> Surely hath Allāh, the Exalted, created people for worship (*ʿibādah*). Thus, the most beloved of Allāh's people are the ones who are most obedient to Him. And the most beloved of acts of obedience to Allāh the Exalted are the those that are purest and most sublime. Let whoever loves sincere devotion (*al-Ikhlāṣ*) to worship, free his heart for Allāh's sake (*li 'l-Lāh*).

Such are the people of *Lām* (*āhlu 'l-Lām*), called the *Lamīyyīn*. They worship Allāh for no reason but Himself, since it was for this purpose that they were they made. Thus, Allāh is enough for them both in this world and the next. Only they can truly relate to the Divine Name of Allāh. For only they have reached the station of servanthood (*ʿubūdīyya*) and can be called *ʿIbādu 'l-Lāh*, servants of Allāh.

Accordingly, Allāh singled out the Prophet Muḥammad ﷺ by giving him the title of *ʿabd* (servant). And that name was beloved by him ﷺ above all the titles that God bestowed on him. In this connection, Ismāʿīl Ḥaqqi al-Bursawī's comments on this *sūra* in his *Rūḥu-l-bayān* are of interest;

> عبد الله هو العبد الذى تحلى بجميع اسمائه فلا يكون فى عباده ارفع
> مقاما واعلى شأنا منه لتحققه بالاسم العظم واتصافه بجميع صفاته
> ولهذا خص نبينا عليه السلام بهذا الاسم فى قوله وانه لما قام عبد الله
> يدعوه فلم يكن هذا الاسم بالحقيقة الا له وللاقطاب من ورثته بتبعيته
> وان اطلق على غيره مجازا

> The ʿAbd Allāh is the servant to whom the theophanies (*tajalīyyat*) of all the names are revealed. There is not among [God's] servants anyone more exalted in station than he nor higher in importance. This is because of his mastery of the greatest name and his being characterized by all the Divine Attributes. For this reason he singled out the Prophet for this name . . . and he called him ʿAbd Allāh (*wa annahu qāma ʿabduhu*) and in reality this name only belongs to him and to the poles (*aqṭāb*) among his inheritors from the *awliyā'* by reason of their subordination to him. If it is applied to others it is by way of metaphor (*majāzan*).

God did not address anyone except the Prophet ﷺ in that way because ʿAbd Allāh names the human being in a state of completedness or perfection. He is the model of humanity for everyone. That is, every quality of servanthood attainable by humankind was first granted to Muḥammad. So, since he ﷺ is the model of humanity, he is the model of servanthood as well.

In sum, one desirous of achieving self-knowledge must acquire knowledge of the Prophet ﷺ. This is the real meaning of

من عرف نفسه فقد عرف ربه

"man ʿarafa nafsahu fa-qad ʿarafa rabbahu" — Whoever knows himself (i.e., his or her soul) hath known his Lord[41] – what we must know is the soul of the Prophet ﷺ. For the Prophet ﷺ announced:

من راني فقد رأى الحق

[41] Al-Imān Abū Sʿad in his *Adab*

"Whoever sees me in his sleep has seen God (*man rā'anī fa-qad rā'a 'l-Ḥaqq*)."[42]

This self-knowledge has a universal destiny. It is meant for all believers' For Allāh says, "For surely hath Allāh bestowed favor on the believers inasmuch as He hath raised a Messenger from themselves."

At the same time, whoever reads the Qur'ān encounters him. So whoever yearns to reach the level of human perfection and become a complete human being, must take on the character of the Qur'ān. If a person's character is not imitative of the Qur'ān, he or she never will achieve the station of *Takhalluq*. That is only for those who want to progress and reach that level. What must they do? They must follow the Qur'ān's commandments and heed its prohibitions. This is the foundation and the beginning.

Whoever wants to reach the level of a perfect human being, created on the image (*ṣūra*) of *al-Raḥmān*, his character must be the Qur'ān. If his character is not al-Qur'ān, never will any human attribute dress him. That is only for those who want to progress and reach that level. What must he or she do? They must first follow what the Qur'ān is ordering him to do and avoid all that it forbids. Are we dong the obligations and leaving the forbidden? Ask yourself.]

Clothed with *akhlāqu 'l-Ḥaqq*, that is, the attributes and names by which Allāh expressed his essence – names like *Ghafūr*, *Rahīm*, *Raḥma* he put on names and attributes different those which possessed by anyone else. That is why Prophet ﷺ has countless names that Allāh gave to him. It is also the reason why Allāh singled him out by giving him the title of *'abd*.

[42] Imam Ahmad.

Accordingly, in verse 3:31 of the Qur'ān the command is issued:

قُلْ إِن كُنتُمْ تُحِبُّونَ اللهَ فَاتَّبِعُونِي يُحْبِبْكُمُ اللهُ

"Say [to them O Muḥammad]: If you love Allāh, then follow me and Allāh will love you."(3:31)

Love is the soul's inclination towards something because of the perfection it perceives in it such that thing will carry it within the proximity it. The one aspiring to servanthood knows that perfection is only from Allāh, belongs to Allāh and exists for the sake of Allāh. Motivated in this way, he naturally follows the Prophet who is the preeminent emblem of God's love of humanity.

The Prophet Muḥammad ﷺ, then, is at once principle (*mabda'*), means (*wasīla*) and end (*gharaḍ*). He is principle because he is the first thing Allāh created from His Light. The *dhāt*, the essence or real nature of his body is made up totally of imperishable light, even though it originated in the dust of the earth. Indeed, because "the *dhāt* of the Prophet has a light that emanates from him, the whole world is filled with his light and there is no place the light of the Prophet does not exist." The Muḥammadan light is in this way "similar to a mirror that fills the entire globe and what is pictured in his *dhāt*."

That is the importance of the name *Sūratu'n-Nūr* that is given to *Sūratu 'l-Ikhlāṣ*. Recall, the Prophet ﷺ said, "Everything has a light and the light of the Qur'ān is '*Qul! Hūwa Allāhu Āḥad*' ('Say! He is Allāh the Unique')" and how there is in his words a veiled reference to himself. For if *Sūratu'n-Nūr* is to the Qur'ān what the pupil of the eye is to man then he himself is to man. Then Muḥammad ﷺ being *al-Insānu 'l-Kāmil* or Perfect Man is like the pupil of the eye of the entire human race. Through it we not only see, we move, we have being (*wujūd*).

Look inside your selves, search inside your souls! Or rather, look to the soul of Muḥammad ﷺ, the perfect model of a human soul. For in another place Allāh makes His meaning explicit,

لَقَدْ جَاءَكُمْ رَسُولٌ مِّنْ أَنفُسِكُمْ

laqad jā'akum rasūlun min anfusikum. . .
"There has come unto you a messenger from among yourselves" (9:128)

That is, "from your own souls." So when tradition says: "*man ʿarafa nafsahu fa-qad ʿarafa rabbahu*" —Whoever knows himself (i.e., his or her soul) hath known his Lord - what we must know is the soul of the Prophet ﷺ. Does not Allāh tell us,

يَا أَيُّهَا الَّذِينَ آمَنُوا اتَّقُوا اللَّهَ وَابْتَغُوا إِلَيْهِ الْوَسِيلَةَ

Yā ayuhā'l-ladhīna āmanū't-aqū'l-Lāha wa'btaghū ilayhi wasīla
"O ye who believe! Be wary of Allāh and seek a means to Him" (5:35)?

The "*wasīlah,*" that is, "the means" is, by general agreement of all the scholars of Islam, the Prophet Muḥammad ﷺ. How could it be otherwise?

But the Prophet ﷺ is also a means because of the command issued in the Qur'ān: "O ye who believe! Be ye wary of Allāh and seek the means (*wasīlah*) to come to Him." By common agreement among interpreters of the Qur'ān the "*wasīla*" or "means to come to Him" referred to in the verse in none other than the Prophet Muḥammad ﷺ.

Finally, the Prophet ﷺ is humanity's final end. That is, we must come to the Prophet ﷺ to achieve our humanity. Put in another, one can say humanity's final end resides in servanthood

(*ʿubūdīyya*). This, in fact, is the basis of God's statement to the Prophet ﷺ in the Qur'ān:

وَلَوْ أَنَّهُمْ إِذ ظَّلَمُوا أَنفُسَهُمْ جَآؤُوكَ فَاسْتَغْفَرُوا اللّهَ وَاسْتَغْفَرَ لَهُمُ الرَّسُولُ

لَوَجَدُوا اللّهَ تَوَّابًا رَّحِيمًا

"When they oppressed themselves, if they had only come unto thee [O Muḥammad!] and asked God's forgiveness, and the Messenger had asked forgiveness for them, they would have found God indeed Oft-returning, Most Merciful." (4:64)

For recognition of *al-Ghafūr* — the One who forgives entails recognition of oneself as the one can receive forgiveness (*al-maghfūr*). Yet, how can such recognition take place without simultaneous recognition of *ar-Raḥmān* (the All-Merciful)?

Similarly, recognition of oneself as one as someone capable of receiving Divine Mercy (*al-marḥūm*) entails not only recognition of *ar-Rabb* or the Lord but also recognition of oneself as *al-marbūb* or the one for whom there can be a Lord. So, recognition of oneself as *maghfūr* and *marḥūm* requires perfect recognition of oneself as *al-marbūb.* And one cannot reach that degree of self-recognition, that is, one for whom there is a Lord, without arrival at the station of *ʿubūdīyya.* Thus, Allāh links servanthood with His mercy and thereby to the Prophet ﷺ who is "*Raḥmatan li 'l-ʿālamīn*" — "A Mercy to the worlds."

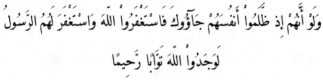

For the Prophet ﷺ alone can be called "servant." That is, he ﷺ alone is servant of Allāh (*ʿAbd Allāh*) by right. In reality, Allāh gave that title only to him. People nowadays call themselves "ʿAbd Allāh," "ʿAbdu 'r-Raḥmān," etc., true enough. But they only do so to imitate the Prophet. For true servanthood is not granted to everyone. And no one else can acquire servanthood in the same sense it was bestowed upon Muḥammad ﷺ.

Servanthood then is a station on the path to Allāh whose end is not a point where the Muslim arrives and then stops. Rather, the journey to servanthood is like approaching a mathematical limit, an ultimate value towards which the believer tends but never quite reaches. Except, he or she has no chance of approaching that limit without inserting functional values drawn from Prophet's ﷺ pure *Sunnah*. For his *Sunnah* is the key of imitating him and therefore, the first step for acquiring servanthood. Even then, the limit of servanthood is never reached but is like a mathematical function approaching infinity.

7

The Virtues of Reciting Sūratu 'l-Ikhlāṣ

حَدَّثَنَا عَبْدُ اللَّهِ بْنُ يُوسُفَ أَخْبَرَنَا مَالِكٌ عَنْ عَبْدِ الرَّحْمَنِ بْنِ عَبْدِ اللَّهِ بْنِ عَبْدِ الرَّحْمَنِ بْنِ أَبِي صَعْصَعَةَ عَنْ أَبِيهِ عَنْ أَبِي سَعِيدٍ الْخُدْرِيِّ أَنَّ رَجُلًا سَمِعَ رَجُلًا يَقْرَأُ قُلْ هُوَ اللَّهُ أَحَدٌ يُرَدِّدُهَا فَلَمَّا أَصْبَحَ جَاءَ إِلَى رَسُولِ اللَّهِ صَلَّى اللَّهُ عَلَيْهِ وَسَلَّمَ فَذَكَرَ ذَلِكَ لَهُ وَكَأَنَّ الرَّجُلَ يَتَقَالُّهَا قَالَ رَسُولُ اللَّهِ صَلَّى اللَّهُ عَلَيْهِ وَسَلَّمَ وَالَّذِي نَفْسِي بِيَدِهِ إِنَّهَا لَتَعْدِلُ ثُلُثَ الْقُرْآنِ

It is related on the authority of Abū Sa'īd al-Khudrī ﷺ that he heard a man reciting *Sūratu 'l-Ikhlāṣ* repeating it over and over again. In the morning he went to the Messenger of Allāh, ﷺ and mentioned it to him, as if he thought little of it. The Messenger of Allāh ﷺ said, "By the One in whose hand my self is, it is equal to one third of the Qur'ān." (Reported by Bukhārī)

حدثنا محمد بن مرزوق البصري أخبرنا حاتم بن ميمون أبو سهل عن ثابت البناني عن أنس بن مالك عن النبي عن النبي صلى الله عليه وسلم

قال: "من قرأ كل يوم مائتي مرة: قل هو الله أحد . محي عنه ذنوبه خمسين سنة الا أن يكون عليه دين"

Anas ؋ reported that the Prophet ﷺ said, "If anyone recites two hundred times daily, "Qul! Hūwa Allāhu Āḥad" the sins of fifty years will be wiped out, unless he is in debt."[43]

وأخرج ابن السني في عمل اليوم والليلة عن عائشة قالت: قال رسول الله صلى الله عليه وسلم: " من قرأ بعد صلاة الجمعة ﴿ قل هو الله أحد ﴾ و ﴿ قل أعوذ برب الفلق ﴾ [الفلق] و ﴿ قل أعوذ برب الناس ﴾ [الناس] سبع مرات أعاذه الله بها من السوء إلى الجمعة الأخرى " .

The Messenger of Allāh ﷺ said:

The one who recites after the Friday prayer 'Qul! Hūwa Allāhu Āḥad,' – 'Say! He is Allāh the One,' [Sūrat al-Ikhlāṣ] Qul a'ūdhu bi Rabbi 'l-Falaq' - 'Say: I seek refuge in the Lord of the daybreak," [Sūrat al-al-Falaq] and 'Qul a'ūdhu bi-rabbi 'n-nās' – 'Say: I seek refuge in the Lord of mankind,' [Sūrat al-an-Nās] seven times, Allāh will protect him from sin until the next Friday. (Ibn as-Sanī in 'Amal al-yawm wa 'l-layl from 'Ā'isha ؋)

---

[43] The ḥadīth is found in at-Tirmidhī narrated it from Anas bin Malik ؋ and ad-Dārimī. The latter version has "fifty times" and does not mention the words "unless he is in debt."

وأخرج ابن النجار في تاريخه عن علي عن رسول الله صلى الله عليه

وسلم قال: " من أراد سفراً فأخذ بعضادتي منزله فقرأ إحدى عشرة

مرة ﴿ قل هو الله أحد ﴾ كان الله له حارساً حتى يرجع"

'Alī ؆ related that the Prophet ؅ said:

> Whoever wishes to travel he should take the
> members of his home and recite over them eleven
> times *Qul Hūwa Allāhu Āḥad*,' Allāh then is a
> Protector for him until he returns.

وأخرج أيضاً عن كعب الأحبار قال: من واظب على قراءة ﴿ قل هو

الله أحد ﴾ وآية الكرسي عشر مرات من ليل أو نهار استوجب

رضوان الله الأكبر، وكان مع أنبيائه، وعصم من الشيطان.

Ka'b al-Ahbār ؆ said:

> Whoever is consistent on the recitation of *Qul Hūwa
> Allāhu Āḥad* and Ayat al-Kursī ten times in the night
> or the day, should expect Allāh's great pleasure; he
> will be with the prophets and he will be protected
> from Satan.

وأخرج أيضاً من طريق دينار عن أنس قال: قال رسول الله صلى الله

عليه وسلم " من قرأ ﴿ قل هو الله أحد ﴾ ألف مرة فقد اشترى

نفسه من الله وهو من خاصة الله " .

Anas related that the Prophet ؅ said:

Whoever recites 'Qul Hūwa Allāhu Āḥad' 1000 times has certainly purchased himself from Allāh and he is among Allāh's special ones.

وأخرج إبراهيم بن محمد الخيارجي في فوائده عن حذيفة قال: قال رسول الله صلى الله عليه وسلم: " من قرأ ﴿ قل هو الله أحد ﴾ ألف مرة فقد اشترى نفسه من الله " .

Hudhayfa ⚘ related that the Prophet ﷺ said:
Whoever recites Qul Hūwa Allāhu Āḥad 1000 times verily has purchased himself from Allāh.

وأخرج البخاري ومسلم والنسائي والبيهقي في الأسماء والصفات عن عائشة " أن النبي صلى الله عليه وسلم بعث رجلاً على سرية، فكان يقرأ لأصحابه في صلاتهم فيختم: بـ ﴿ قل هو الله أحد ﴾ فلما رجعوا ذكروا ذلك لرسول الله صلى الله عليه وسلم فقال: " سلوه لأي شيء يصنع ذلك؟ " فسألوه فقال: لأنها صفة الرحمن، فأنا أحب أن أقرأها . فأتوا النبي صلى الله عليه وسلم، فأخبروه فقال: " أخبروه أن الله تعالى يحبه "

It is related from 'Ā'isha ⚘ that the Prophet ﷺ sent a man on an expedition. And he used to recite in his prayer with his companions and end with Qul Hūwa Allāhu Āḥad, and when they returned they mentioned that before the Prophet of Allāh ﷺ and he said, "Ask him which then caused him to do that?" They asked him and he said, "Because it is an Attribute of the Merciful, and truly I love to recite it." They came to the Prophet ﷺ and informed him of this and he ﷺ said, "Inform him that Allāh loves him."

وأخرج ابن الضريس عن أنس قال: " قال رجل لرسول الله صلى الله عليه وسلم: إن لي أخاً قد حبب إليه قراءة ﴿ قل هو الله أحد ﴾ فقال: " بشر أخاك بالجنة ".

Anas ؓ related that a man said to the Prophet of Allāh ﷺ "Indeed I have a brother and indeed it is beloved to him to recite *Qul Hūwa Allāhu Āḥad*, and he ﷺ said, "Give him good tidings to your brother of Paradise."

وأخرج عبد الرزاق وابن أبي شيبة وابن ماجة وابن الضريس عن بريدة قال: " دخلت مع رسول الله صلى الله عليه وسلم المسجد ويدي في يده، فإذا رجل يصلي يقول: اللهم إني أسألك بأنك أنت الله لا إله إلا أنت الواحد الأحد الصمد الذي لم يلد ولم يولد ولم يكن له كفواً أحد، فقال رسول الله صلى الله عليه وسلم: " لقد دعا الله باسمه الأعظم الذي إذا سئل به أعطى وإذا دعي به أجاب " .

It was related from Burayda ؓ who said:

> I entered the mosque with the Prophet of Allāh ﷺ and my hand was in his hand. There was a man praying and he said, "O Allāh, truly I ask of You in that You are Allāh, there is no god except You, the One, the Unique, the Eternal, Who begets not nor is He begotten and there is like Him no one." Then the Prophet of Allāh ﷺ said, "Indeed he has prayed to Allāh with His Greatest Name which, if one asks by means of is granted and if one prays with it is answered."

وأخرج أبو نعيم في الحلية عن أبي غالب مولى خالد بن عبدالله قال: قال عمر ذات ليلة قبيل الصبح يا أبا غالب ألا تقوم فتصلي، ولو تقرأ بثلث القرآن، فقلت: قد دنا الصبح فكيف أقرأ بثلث القرآن فقال: إن رسول الله صلى الله عليه وسلم قال: " إن سورة الإخلاص ﴿ قل هو الله أحد ﴾ تعدل ثلث القرآن ".

Abū Ghālib, the servant of Khālid bin ʿAbdullāh ؓ said:

> One night close to dawn ʿUmar ؓ said, "O Abā Ghālib! Will you not stand and pray, even if you recite one third of the Quran?" So I said, "Truly the dawn has come down, so how will I recite with one third of the Quran?" So he said, "Indeed the Prophet of Allāh ﷺ said, 'Indeed *Sūratu 'l-Ikhlāṣ* [*Qul Hūwa Allāhu Āḥad*] equals one third of the Quran."

وأخرج ابن الضريس عن سعيد بن المسيب قال: " كان رجل من أصحاب رسول الله صلى الله عليه وسلم يقال له معاوية، فخرج رسول الله صلى الله عليه وسلم في غزوة تبوك، وهو مريض ثقيل، فسار رسول الله صلى الله عليه وسلم عشرة أيام ثم لقيه جبريل فقال: إن معاوية بن معاوية توفي، فحزن رسول الله صلى الله عليه وسلم فقال: أيسرك أن أريك قبره؟ قال: نعم، فضرب بجناحه الأرض، فلم يبق جبل إلا انخفض حتى أبدى الله قبره فكبر رسول الله صلى الله عليه وسلم وجبريل عن يمينه وصفوف الملائكة سبعين ألفاً حتى إذا فرغ من صلاته قال: يا جبريل بم نزل معاوية بن معاوية من الله بهذه المنزلة؟ قال: بـ ﴿ قل هو الله أحد ﴾ كان يقرأها قائماً وقاعداً وماشياً ونائماً، ولقد كنت أخاف على أمتك حتى نزلت هذه السورة فيها ".

Saʿīd ibn al-Musayyib ﷺ said:

> There was a man from the Companions of the Prophet ﷺ, whom they called Muʿawīyah. The Prophet set out in the Battle of Tabūk and that man was gravely ill. So the Prophet ﷺ went for ten days then Jibrīl met him and said, "Muʿawiyah ibn Muʿawiyah passed away." The Prophet ﷺ was saddened and said, "Is it easy (to show me his grave?" He said, "Yes," then he hit the earth with his wing. Then there did not remain any mountain

> [between him and the grave] except it shrank until Allāh revealed his grave. Then the Prophet made the *takbīr* [of ṣalāt al-janāzah] and Jibrīl was on his right, and 70,000 rows of angels were in attendance. When he ﷺ had completed his prayers he said, "O Jibrīl, why was Muʿawiyah ibn Muʿawiyah granted to attain such a rank from Allāh?" He said, "With *Qul Hūwa Allāhu Āḥad*. He used to recite it standing and sitting and walking and sleeping. And truly I used to fear for your Community until this sūrah was revealed during it."

وأخرج ابن عدي والبيهقي في الشعب عن أنس رضي الله عنه أن رسول الله صلى الله عليه وسلم قال: " من قرأ ﴿ قل هو الله أحد ﴾ مائتي مرة غفر له خطيئة خمسين سنة إذا اجتنب أربع خصال الدماء والأموال والفروج والأشربة " .

Anas related that the Prophet ﷺ said:

> Whoever recites *Qul Hūwa Allāhu Āḥad* one hundred times will be forgiven the sins of fifty years as long as he has avoided four characteristics: shedding blood, [stealing] wealth, fornication and adultery, and drink.

وأخرج ابن عدي والبيهقي في الشعب عن أنس رضي الله عنه أن النبي صلى الله عليه وسلم قال: " من قرأ ﴿ قل هو الله أحد ﴾ على طهارة مائة مرة كطهارة الصلاة يبدأ بفاتحة الكتاب كتب الله له بكل

حرف عشر حسنات، ومحا عنه عشر سيّئات، ورفع له عشر درجات،

وبنى له مائة قصر في الجنة وكأنما قرأ القرآن ثلاثاً وثلاثين مرة، وهي براءة

من الشرك، ومحضرة للملائكة، ومنفرة للشياطين، ولها دويّ حول العرش

تذكر بصاحبها حتى ينظر الله إليه، وإذا نظر إليه لم يعذبه أبداً ".

Anas ❀ related that the Prophet ﷺ said:

> Whoever recites *Qul Hūwa Allāhu Āḥad* one
> hundred times while in a state of ritual purity
> (*wuḍū*) like that required for prayers, beginning
> with the Opening of the Book, Allāh will write for
> each letter ten virtues (*ḥasanāt*) and erase from him
> ten sins, and raise him up ten levels and build for
> him 100 palaces in the Garden and it will be as if he
> had recited the Quran 33 times. And it will be
> freedom from association with Allāh (*shirk*), and it
> will be the presence of angels (*maḥḍarat al-malā'ikat*)
> and the cause of devils to flee [from him] and it
> makes an echoing roar around the Throne that
> mentions the one reciting it until Allāh gazes upon
> him. And if Allāh gazes upon him then he will
> never be punished, ever."

وأخرج أبو يعلى عن جابر بن عبدالله قال: قال رسول الله صلى الله

عليه وسلم: " ثلاث من جاء بهن مع الإيمان دخل من أي أبواب الجنة

شاء، وزوج من الحور العين حيث شاء، من عفا عن قاتله، وأدى ديناً

خفياً، وقرأ في دبر كل صلاة مكتوبة عشر مرات ﴿ قل هو الله أحد

﴾ فقال أبو بكر: أو إحداهن يا رسول الله؟ قال: " أو إحداهن "

From Jābir ibn ‘Abd Allāh ۞ who said, the Prophet ۞ said:

> There are three things, whoever comes with them possessing faith, enters the Garden from whichever gate he wishes and will marry from the Ḥūr al-‘Ayn[44] as he likes: the one who forgave his killer; the one who gives a loan secretly and the one who recited at the end of every obligatory prayer *Qul Hūwa Allāhu Āḥad* ten times. Then Abū Bakr said, "Or one of these, O Prophet of Allāh?" He replied, "Or one of them."

وأخرج الطبراني عن جرير البجلي قال: قال رسول الله صلى الله عليه

وسلم: " من قرأ ﴿ قل هو الله أحد ﴾ حين يدخل منزله نفت الفقر

من أهل ذلك المنزل والجيران " .

Jarīr al-Bajalī ۞ related that the Prophet ۞ said:

> Whoever recited *Qul Hūwa Allāhu Āḥad* at the time of entering his home, poverty will be repelled from the family of that home and from that of the neighbors.

---

[44] Virtuous maidens of Paradise, representing the Lord's Beauty Oceans.

وأخرج الطبراني في الأوسط وأبو نعيم في الحلية بسند ضعيف عن
عبدالله بن الشخير قال: قال رسول الله صلى الله عليه وسلم: " من قرأ
﴿ قل هو الله أحد ﴾ في مرضه الذي يموت فيه لم يفتن في قبره، وأمن
من فتنه القبر، وحملته الملائكة يوم القيامة بأكفها حتى تجيزه الصراط إلى
الجنة " .

From 'Abd Allāh ibn ash-Shakhīr ❀ who related that the Prophet
❀ said:

> Whoever recites *Qul Hūwa Allāhu Āḥad* during the
> illness from which he dies, will not be tried in the
> grave and will be secure from the trial of the grave
> and the angels will carry him in their palms on the
> Day of Rising, to convey him across the Bridge
> until he enters Paradise.

وأخرج سعيد بن منصور وابن الضريس عن علي قال: من قرأ ﴿ قل
هو الله أحد ﴾ عشر مرار بعد الفجر وفي لفظ، في دبر الغداة لم يلحق
به ذلك اليوم ذنب، وإن جهد الشيطان .

'Alī ❀ said:

> Whoever recites *Qul Hūwa Allāhu Āḥad* ten times
> after Fajr (and in one version in the middle of noon)
> will not encounter a single sin on that day; even if
> Shayṭān were to strive [to make him sin].

وأخرج ابن أبي شيبة والبخاري وأبو داود والترمذي والنسائي وابن ماجة عن عائشة أن النبي صلى الله عليه وسلم كان إذا أوى إلى فراشه كل ليلة جمع كفيه ثم نفث فيهما فقرأ فيهما ﴿ قل هو الله أحد ﴾ و ﴿ قل أعوذ برب الفلق ﴾ [سورة الفلق] و ﴿ قل أعوذ برب الناس ﴾ [سورة الناس] ثم يمسح بهما ما استطاع من جسده. يبدأ بهما على رأسه ووجهه وما أقبل من جسده، يفعل ذلك ثلاث مرات.

When the Prophet ﷺ took himself to bed every night would put his palms together and then blow into them, and then he would recite into them *Qul Hūwa Allāhu Āḥad* and *Qul aʿūdhu bi Rabbi 'l-Falaq* and *Qul aʿūdhu bi-rabbi 'n-nās.* Then he would wipe whatever he was able from his body begining on top of his head, then over his face and whatever he could reach from his body. He would do that three times.

وأخرج ابن سعد وعبد بن حميد وأبو داود والترمذي وصححه والنسائي وعبد الله بن أحمد في زوائد الزهد والطبراني عن عبد الله بن حبيب أن النبي صلى الله عليه وسلم قال له: " اقرأ ﴿ قل هو الله أحد ﴾ والمعوّذتين حين تصبح وحين تمسي ثلاثاً يكفيك من كل شيء ".

From ʿAbd Allāh ibn Ḥabīb ؓ that the Prophet ﷺ said to him:

Recite *Qul Hūwa Allāhu Āḥad* and the two chapters of Refuge in the morn and evening three times, it will suffice you from everything.

وأخرج ابن مردويه والبيهقي في الشعب عن علي قال: " بينا رسول الله صلى الله عليه وسلم ذات ليلة يصلي فوضع يده على الأرض لدغته عقرب فتناولها رسول الله صلى الله عليه وسلم بنعله فقتلها، فلما انصرف قال: " لعن الله العقرب ما تدع مصلياً ولا غيره أو نبياً أو غيره " ثم دعا بملح وماء فجعله في إناء، ثم جعل يصبه على إصبعه حيث لدغته ويمسحها ويعوذها بالمعوذتين، وفي لفظ فجعل يمسح عليها ويقرأ ﴿ قل هو الله أحد ﴾ و ﴿ قل أعوذ برب الفلق ﴾ و ﴿ قل أعوذ برب الناس ﴾ " .

'Alī ﷺ said:

> The Prophet ﷺ was with us one night when he placed his hand on the earth and a scorpion bit him and the Prophet ﷺ hit it with his sandal and killed it. When he had finished his prayers he said, "Allāh has cursed the scorpion for it does not leave alone a person who is praying nor anyone else; nor a prophet, nor anyone else." He then called for salt and water and put them in a bowl and then he started pouring it over the fingers where he had been bitten wiping them and while seeking refuge from [its poison] by means of the two Chapters of Refuge. (And in another version 'and he wiped

over them while *reciting Qul Hūwa Allāhu Āḥad, Qul a'ūdhū bi Rabbi 'l-Falaq* and *Qul a'ūdhū bi-rabbi 'n-nās')."*

وأخرج ابن المنذر وابن أبي حاتم وأبو الشيخ في العظمة والبيهقي في الأسماء والصفات من طريق علي عن ابن عباس قال: الصمد السيد الذي قد كمل في سؤدده، والشريف الذي قد كمل في شرفه، والعظيم الذي قد كمل في عظمته، والحليم الذي قد كمل في حلمه، والغني الذي قد كمل في غناه، والجبار الذي قد كمل في جبروته، والعالم الذي قد كمل في علمه، والحكيم الذي قد كمل في حكمته، وهو الذي قد كمل في أنواع الشرف والسؤدد، وهو الله سبحانه هذه صفته لا تنبغي إلا له، ليس كفو، وليس كمثله شيء.

It was related by way of 'Alī ﷺ from Ibn 'Abbas ﷺ who said:

Aṣ-Ṣamad is The Master Who is perfect in His Masterhood and The Noble Who is perfect in His Nobility, and The Great One Who is perfect in His Greatness, and The Forbearing, Who is perfect in His Forbearance and the Rich who is perfect in His Richness, and The Overwhelming One, Who is perfect in His overwhelming, and The Knower Who is perfect in His Knowledge, and The Wise Who is perfect in His Wisdom and He is the One Who is perfect in different aspects of Nobility and Mastership and He is Allāh, Exalted be He, and these Attributes are not permitted except to Him.

Nothing is comparable to Him and there is nothing like unto Him.

حَدَّثَنَا أَبُو عَامِرٍ، حَدَّثَنَا مَالِكٌ، عَنْ عَبْدِ اللَّهِ بْنِ عَبْدِ الرَّحْمَنِ، عَنِ ابْنِ حُنَيْنٍ، عَنْ أَبِي هُرَيْرَةَ، أَنَّ النَّبِيَّ صَلَّى اللَّهُ عَلَيْهِ وَسَلَّمَ سَمِعَ رَجُلًا يَقْرَأُ قُلْ هُوَ اللَّهُ أَحَدٌ فَقَالَ وَجَبَتْ قَالُوا يَا رَسُولَ اللَّهِ مَا وَجَبَتْ قَالَ وَجَبَتْ لَهُ الْجَنَّةُ

Abū Hurayra ﷺ said, "I was going along with the Messenger of Allāh ﷺ when he heard a man reciting *Sūratu 'l-Ikhlāṣ*. The Messenger of Allāh, ﷺ, said, "It is obligatory," and I asked him, "What is, Messenger of Allāh?" ﷺ and he said, "The Garden." I wanted to tell the man the good news but I was afraid that I would miss the midday meal with the Messenger of Allāh ﷺ and I preferred to eat with the Messenger of Allāh ﷺ. When I went to the man afterwards I found that he had gone."

وعن سهيل ابن سعد رضى الله عنه جاء رجل الى النبى عليه السلام وشكا اليه الفقر فقال اذا دخلت بيتك فسلم ان كان فيه احد وان لم يكن فيه احد فسلم على نفسك واقرأ قل هو الله احد مرة واحدة ففعل الرجل ذلك فأدر الله عليه رزقا حتى افاض على جيرانه

A man came to the Prophet ﷺ and complained of poverty. The Prophet ﷺ said, "Whenever you enter your house say "*as-salāmu 'alaykum.*" If someone is there say it to them. And if not, then say it to yourself. Then, recite one time *Sūratu 'l-Ikhlās*." The man did that and Allāh provided him so much provision that he was able to help his neighbors.

Printed in the United States
58532LVS00008B/205-285

9 781930 409422